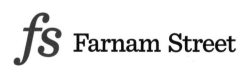

Farnam Street is devoted to helping you develop an understanding of how the world really works, make better decisions, and live a better life. We address such topics as mental models, decision-making, learning, reading, and the art of living.

In a world full of noise, Farnam Street is a place where you can step back and think about time-tested ideas while asking yourself questions that lead to meaningful understanding. We cover ideas from science and the humanities that will not only expand your intellectual horizons but also help you connect ideas, think in multidisciplinary ways, and explore meaning.

Headquartered in Ottawa, Canada, and run by Shane Parrish, we operate around the globe and have helped millions of people master the best of what other people have already figured out.

The quality of your thinking depends on the models that are in your head.

This is a statement we strongly believe in at Farnam Street. This conviction drives much of what we do.

When you learn to see the world as it is, and not as you want it to be, everything changes. The solution to any problem becomes more apparent when you can view it through more than one lens. You'll be able to spot opportunities you couldn't see before, avoid costly mistakes that may be holding you back, and begin to make meaningful progress in your life.

That's the power of mental models. And that's why we created the Great Mental Models project.

The Great Mental Models Project is a labor of love to help equalize opportunity in the world by making a high-quality, multidisciplinary, interconnected education free and available to everyone.

That's a big ambition. And we're glad we don't have to shoulder the burden alone. Automattic, an amazing company dedicated to giving great ideas a voice and a global platform, shares our vision and wanted to help. They've offered to sponsor the printing of this book so it can get into more hands and positively influence the way more people see the world. We're grateful for their support. (Check out their Afterthoughts on page 183.)

Along with the books, we're developing additional tools and resources to help readers more readily connect the models in their heads, so their use becomes second nature. By purchasing this book, you make it possible for us to continue our efforts and see this initiative through to completion. Thank you for your support. If you'd like to learn more about the Great Mental Models project, **please visit FS.blog/tgmm**

Published in 2019 by Latticework Publishing Inc.
99 Fifth Avenue, #22, Ottawa, ON K1S 5K4
Copyright © Farnam Street Media Inc.
Creative Direction by Morgwn Rimel
Designed and typeset by FLOK, Berlin
Illustrations by Marcia Mihotich, London
Printed in Latvia by Livonia Print

A portion of this work has appeared online at fs.blog.

www.fs.blog

ISBN: 978-1-9994490-0-1

The Great
Mental Models
Vol.1

General Thinking Concepts

Contents

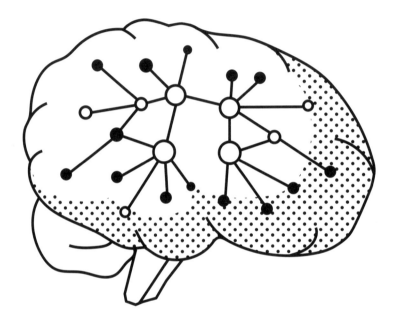

The key to better understanding the world is to build
a latticework of mental models.

Preface

Education doesn't prepare you for the real world. At least, it didn't prepare me. I was two weeks into my job at an intelligence agency on September 11, 2001 when the world suddenly changed. The job I had been hired to do was no longer the one that was needed. I had a computer science degree; I came from a world of 1s and 0s, not people, families, and interpersonal dynamics. I was thrust into a series of promotions for which I had received no guidance, that came with responsibilities I had no idea how to navigate. Now I found that my decisions affected not only my employees but their families. Not only my country, but other countries. The only problem? I had no idea how to make decisions. I only knew I had an obligation to make the best decisions I could.

To improve my ability to make decisions, I looked around and found some mentors. I watched them carefully and learned from them. I read everything I could about making decisions. I even took some time off work to go back to school and earn my MBA, hoping that I would finally learn how to make better decisions, as if that was some end state rather than a constantly evolving journey.

My belief that the MBA program was a good use of my time was eroded fairly quickly. When I showed up to write an exam only to find out it was an open book test, I realized my expectations were entirely wrong and in need of updating. Was I in a master's program or grade school? Some days, I couldn't tell. And yet that is where everything changed for me.

I realized that I couldn't fail as long as I knew where the answers were in the books I could bring to the exams. This was actually quite liberating. I stopped putting effort into my assignments and started learning about someone who was casually mentioned in class. That person was Charlie Munger.[*] I went from theoretical examples that

[*] Munger, Charlie (Charles), 1924 - American investor, businessman and philanthropist. Vice-Chairman of Berkshire Hathaway. Avid proponent that elementary, worldly wisdom and high ethical standards are required in business.

were completely divorced from the real world, to the wisdom behind the achievements of one of the most successful businessmen of all time. Munger, who you will come to know in these volumes, is the billionaire business partner of Warren Buffett[*] at Berkshire Hathaway. He's easy to like: intelligent, witty, and irreverent. Finding Munger opened the door to unexpected intellectual pleasure. I felt like I had finally found knowledge that was useful because it was gained from someone's real effort to better understand how the world works. It was so much more satisfying to learn from someone who had tried to put many theories into practice and was willing to share his results. The fact that Munger was so professionally successful made it all the more compelling.

Munger has a way of thinking through problems using what he calls a broad latticework of mental models. These are chunks of knowledge from different disciplines that can be simplified and applied to better understand the world. The way he describes it, they help identify what information is relevant in any given situation, and the most reasonable parameters to work in. His track record shows that this doesn't just make sense in theory but is devastatingly useful in practice. I started writing about my learnings, the result being the website fs.blog. The last eight years of my life have been devoted to identifying and learning the mental models that have the greatest positive impact, and trying to understand how we think, how we update, how we learn, and how we can make better decisions.

I joke with my kids that if you want to suck up someone's brain, you should simply read a book. All the great wisdom of humanity is written down somewhere. When we were talking about mental models one day the kids asked if we had *the* mental models book. This made me pause, and I was struck with the realization that such a book didn't exist. I didn't have something I could share with my kids, and that was a problem. A very solvable problem.

*
Buffett, Warren, 1930 - American investor, businessman and philanthropist. Chairman and CEO of Berkshire Hathaway. Often referred to as "the Oracle of Omaha", he is considered one of the most successful investors in the world.

1
Feynman, Richard.
The Pleasure of Finding Things Out:
The Best Short Works of Richard
P. Feynman. New York: Perseus
Publishing, 1999.

This book, and the volumes which will follow, are the books I wish had existed years ago when I started learning about mental models. These are my homage to the idea that we can benefit from understanding how the world works and applying that understanding to keep us out of trouble.

The ideas in these volumes are not my own, nor do I deserve any credit for them. They come from the likes of Charlie Munger, Nassim Taleb, Charles Darwin, Peter Kaufman, Peter Bevelin, Richard Feynman, Albert Einstein, and so many others. As the Roman poet Publius Terentius wrote: "Nothing has yet been said that's not been said before." I've only curated, edited, and shaped the work of others before me.

The timeless, broad ideas in these volumes are for my children and their children and their children's children. In creating them, I hope to allow others to approach problems with clarity and confidence, helping to make their journey through life more successful and rewarding.

« You only think you know, as a matter of fact. And most of your actions are based on incomplete knowledge and you really don't know what it is all about, or what the purpose of the world is, or know a great deal of other things. It is possible to live and not know. »

Richard Feynman [1]

Acquiring Wisdom

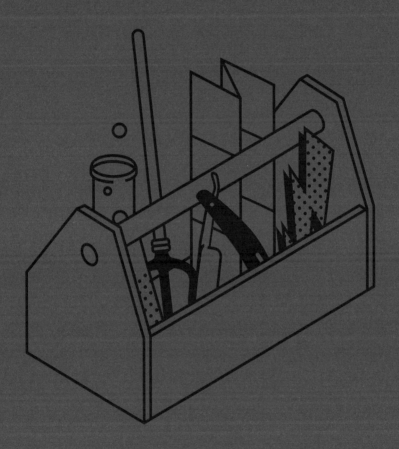

You're only as good as your tools.

I believe in the
discipline of
mastering the best
of what other people
have figured out.

Charlie Munger[1]

Introduction: Acquiring Wisdom

In life and business, the person with the fewest blind spots wins. Removing blind spots means we see, interact with, and move closer to understanding reality. We think better. And thinking better is about finding simple processes that help us work through problems from multiple dimensions and perspectives, allowing us to better choose solutions that fit what matters to us. The skill for finding the right solutions for the right problems is one form of wisdom.

This book is about the pursuit of that wisdom, the pursuit of uncovering how things work, the pursuit of going to bed smarter than when we woke up. It is a book about getting out of our own way so we can understand how the world really is. Decisions based on improved understanding will be better than ones based on ignorance. While we can't predict which problems will inevitably crop up in life, we can learn time-tested ideas that help us prepare for whatever the world throws at us.

Perhaps more importantly, this book is about *avoiding* problems. This often comes down to understanding a problem accurately and seeing the secondary and subsequent consequences of any proposed action. The author and explorer of mental models, Peter Bevelin, put it best: "I don't want to be a great problem solver. I want to avoid problems—prevent them from happening and doing it right from the beginning." [2]

How can we do things right from the beginning?

We must understand how the world works and adjust our behavior accordingly. Contrary to what we're led to believe, thinking better isn't about being a genius. It is about the processes we use to uncover reality and the choices we make once we do.

1
Munger, Charles.
Worldly Wisdom Revisited. Lecture and dialogue presented at Stanford Law School, Stanford, CA, December 29, 1997.

2
Parrish, Shane.
Peter Bevelin on Seeking Wisdom, Mental Models, Learning, and a Lot More. Farnam Street Blog. Retrieved from: https://www.fs.blog/2016/10/peter-bevelin-seeking-wisdom-mental-models/

How this book can help you

This is the first of a series of volumes aimed at defining and exploring the Great Mental Models—those that have the broadest utility across our lives. Mental models describe the way the world works. They shape how we think, how we understand, and how we form beliefs. Largely subconscious, mental models operate below the surface. We're not generally aware of them and yet they're the reason when we look at a problem we consider some factors relevant and others irrelevant. They are how we infer causality, match patterns, and draw analogies. They are how we think and reason.

A mental model is simply a representation of how something works. We cannot keep all of the details of the world in our brains, so we use models to simplify the complex into understandable and organizable chunks. Whether we realize it or not, we then use these models every day to think, decide, and understand our world. While there are millions of mental models, some true and some false, these volumes will focus on the ones with the greatest utility—the all-star team of mental models.

Volume One presents the first nine models, general thinking concepts. Although these models are hiding in plain sight, they are useful tools that you were likely never directly taught. Put to proper use, they will improve your understanding of the world we live in and improve your ability to look at a situation through different lenses, each of which reveals a different layer. They can be used in a wide variety of situations and are essential to making rational decisions, even when there is no clear path. Collectively they will allow you to walk around any problem in a three-dimensional way.

Our approach to the Great Mental Models rests on the idea that the fundamentals of knowledge are available to everyone. There is no discipline that is off limits—the core ideas from all fields of study contain principles that reveal how the universe works, and are therefore essential to navigating it.

Our models come from fundamental disciplines that most of us have never studied, but no prior knowledge is required—only a sharp mind with a desire to learn.

Why mental models?

There is no system that can prepare us for all risks. Factors of chance introduce a level of complexity that is not entirely predictable. But being able to draw on a repertoire of mental models can help us minimize risk by understanding the forces that are at play. Likely consequences don't have to be a mystery.

Not having the ability to shift perspective by applying knowledge from multiple disciplines makes us vulnerable. Mistakes can become catastrophes whose effects keep compounding, creating stress and limiting our choices. Multidisciplinary thinking, learning these mental models and applying them across our lives, creates less stress and more freedom. The more we can draw on the diverse knowledge contained in these models, the more solutions will present themselves.

Understanding reality

Understanding reality is a vague phrase, one you've already encountered as you've read this book. Of course we want to understand reality, but how? And why is it important?

In order to see a problem for what it is, we must first break it down into its substantive parts so the interconnections can reveal themselves. This bottom-up perspective allows us to expose what we believe to be the causal relationships and how they will govern the situation both now and in the future. Being able to accurately describe the full scope of a situation is the first step to understanding it.

Using the lenses of our mental models helps us illuminate these interconnections. The more lenses used on a given problem, the more of reality reveals itself. The more of reality we see, the more we understand. The more we understand, the more we know what to do.

To defeat Antaeus, Heracles separated him from
the source of his power.

1
Graves, Robert.
The Greek Myths. The Folio Society:
London, 1996 (first published in
1955)

2
Bulfinch, Thomas.
The Golden Age of Myth and Legend.
UK: Wordsworth Editions, 1993.

Simple and well-defined problems won't need many lenses, as the variables that matter are known. So too are the interactions between them. In such cases we generally know what to do to get the intended results with the fewest side effects possible. When problems are more complicated, however, the value of having a brain full of lenses becomes readily apparent.

That's not to say all lenses (or models) apply to all problems. They don't. And it's not to say that having more lenses (or models) will be an advantage in all problems. It won't. This is why learning and applying the Great Mental Models is a process that takes some work. But the truth is, most problems are multidimensional, and thus having more lenses often offers significant help with the problems we are facing.

Keeping your feet on the ground

In Greek mythology, Antaeus was the human-giant son of Poseidon, god of the sea, and Gaia, Mother Earth. Antaeus had a strange habit. He would challenge all those who passed through his country to a wrestling match. Greek wrestling isn't much different from what we think of today when we think of wrestling. The goal is to force the opponent to the ground. Antaeus always won and his opponents' skulls were used to build a temple to his father. While Antaeus was undefeated and nearly undefeatable, there was a catch to his invulnerability. His epic strength depended on constant contact with the earth. When he lost touch with earth, he lost all of his strength.

On the way to the Garden of the Hesperides, Heracles was to fight Antaeus as one of his 12 labors. After a few rounds in which Heracles flung the giant to the ground only to watch him revive, he realized he could not win by using traditional wrestling techniques. Instead, Heracles fought to lift him off the ground. Away from contact with his mother, Antaeus lost his strength and Heracles crushed him.[1,2]

1
Wallace, David Foster,
This Is Water: Some Thoughts,
Delivered on a Significant Occasion,
about Living a Compassionate Life.
New York: Little Brown and
Company, 2009.

When understanding is separated from reality, we lose our powers. Understanding must constantly be tested against reality and updated accordingly. This isn't a box we can tick, a task with a definite beginning and end, but a continuous process.

You all know the person who has all the answers on how to improve your organization, or the friend who has the cure to world hunger. While pontificating with friends over a bottle of wine at dinner is fun, it won't help you improve. The only way you'll know the extent to which you understand reality is to put your ideas and understanding into action. If you don't test your ideas against the real world—keep contact with the earth— how can you be sure you understand?

Getting in our own way

The biggest barrier to learning from contact with reality is ourselves. It's hard to understand a system that we are part of because we have blind spots, where we can't see what we aren't looking for, and don't notice what we don't notice.

«There are these two young fish swimming along and they happen to meet an older fish swimming the other way, who nods at them and says "Morning, boys. How's the water?" And the two young fish swim on for a bit, and then eventually one of them looks over at the other and goes "What the hell is water?"»

David Foster Wallace [1]

Our failures to update from interacting with reality spring primarily from three things: not having the right perspective or vantage point, ego-induced denial, and distance from the consequences of our decisions. As we will learn in greater

*
Galilei, Galileo.
1564-1642 - Italian polymath. He
made significant contributions
to astronomy, physics, and
engineering and is thought of by
many as the father of modern
science. His brilliance continues to
inspire and references to him can
be found in many places, including
songs by Queen and the Indigo Girls.

detail throughout the volumes on mental models, these can all get in the way. They make it easier to keep our existing and flawed beliefs than to update them accordingly. Let's briefly flesh these out:

The first flaw is perspective. We have a hard time seeing any system that we are in. Galileo* had a great analogy to describe the limits of our default perspective. Imagine you are on a ship that has reached constant velocity (meaning without a change in speed or direction). You are below decks and there are no portholes. You drop a ball from your raised hand to the floor. To you, it looks as if the ball is dropping straight down, thereby confirming gravity is at work.

Now imagine you are a fish (with special x-ray vision) and you are watching this ship go past. You see the scientist inside, dropping a ball. You register the vertical change in the position of the ball. But you are also able to see a horizontal change. As the ball was pulled down by gravity it also shifted its position east by about 20 feet. The ship moved through the water and therefore so did the ball. The scientist on board, with no external point of reference, was not able to perceive this horizontal shift.

This analogy shows us the limits of our perception. We must be open to other perspectives if we truly want to understand the results of our actions. Despite feeling that we've got all the information, if we're on the ship, the fish in the ocean has more he can share.

The second flaw is ego. Many of us tend to have too much invested in our opinions of ourselves to see the world's feedback—the feedback we need to update our beliefs about reality. This creates a profound ignorance that keeps us banging our head against the wall over and over again. Our inability to learn from the world because of our ego happens for many reasons, but two are worth mentioning here. First, we're so afraid about what others will say about us that we fail to put our ideas out there and subject them to criticism. This way we can always be right. Second, if we do put our ideas out there and they are criticized, our ego steps in to protect us. We become invested in defending instead of upgrading our ideas.

The third flaw is distance. The further we are from the results of our decisions, the easier it is to keep our current views rather than update them. When you put your hand on a hot stove, you quickly learn the natural consequence. You pay the price for your mistakes. Since you are a pain-avoiding creature, you update your view. Before you touch another stove, you check to see if it's hot. But you don't just learn a micro lesson that applies in one situation. Instead, you draw a general abstraction, one that tells you to check before touching anything that could potentially be hot.

Organizations over a certain size often remove us from the direct consequences of our decisions. When we make decisions that other people carry out, we are one or more levels removed and may not immediately be able to update our understanding. We come a little off the ground, if you will. The further we are from the feedback of the decisions, the easier it is to convince ourselves that we are right and avoid the challenge, the pain, of updating our views.

Admitting that we're wrong is tough. It's easier to fool ourselves that we're right at a high level than at the micro level, because at the micro level we see and feel the immediate consequences. When we touch that hot stove, the feedback is powerful and instantaneous. At a high or macro level we are removed from the immediacy of the situation, and our ego steps in to create a narrative that suits what we want to believe, instead of what really happened.

These flaws are the main reasons we keep repeating the same mistakes, and why we need to keep our feet on the ground as much as we can. As Confucius said, "A man who has committed a mistake and doesn't correct it, is committing another mistake."

1
Benoit, Andy,
"The Case for the...Broncos."
Sports Illustrated, January 13,
2014.

The majority of the time, we don't even perceive what conflicts with our beliefs. It's much easier to go on thinking what we've already been thinking than go through the pain of updating our existing, false beliefs. When it comes to seeing what is—that is, understanding reality—we can follow Charles Darwin's advice to notice things "which easily escape attention," and ask why things happened.

We also tend to undervalue the elementary ideas and overvalue the complicated ones. Most of us get jobs based on some form of specialized knowledge, so this makes sense. We don't think we have much value if we know the things everyone else does, so we focus our effort on developing unique expertise to set ourselves apart. The problem is then that we reject the simple to make sure what we offer can't be contributed by someone else. But simple ideas are of great value because they can help us prevent complex problems.

In identifying the Great Mental Models we have looked for elementary principles, the ideas from multiple disciplines that form a time-tested foundation. It may seem counterintuitive, to work on developing knowledge that is available to everyone, but the universe works in the same way no matter where you are in it. What you need is to understand the principles, so that when the details change you are still able to identify what is really going on. This is part of what makes the Great Mental Models so valuable—understanding the principles, you can easily change tactics to apply the ones you need.

« Most geniuses—especially those who lead others—prosper not by deconstructing intricate complexities but by exploiting unrecognized simplicities. »

Andy Benoit [1]

These elementary ideas, so often overlooked, are from multiple disciplines: biology, physics, chemistry, and more. These help us understand the interconnections of the world, and see it for how it really is. This understanding allows us to develop causal relationships, which allow us to match patterns, which allow us to draw analogies. All of this so we can navigate reality with more clarity and comprehension of the real dynamics involved.

Understanding is not enough

However, understanding reality is not everything. The pursuit of understanding fuels meaning and adaptation, but this understanding, by itself, is not enough.

Understanding only becomes useful when we adjust our behavior and actions accordingly. The Great Models are not just theory. They are actionable insights that can be used to effect positive change in your life. What good is it to know that you constantly interrupt people if you fail to adjust your behavior in light of this? In fact, if you know and don't change your behavior it often has a negative effect. People around you will tell themselves the simplest story that makes sense to them given what they see: that you just don't care. Worse still, because you understand that you interrupt people, you're surprised when you get the same results over and over. Why? You've failed to reflect on your new understanding and adjust your behavior.

In the real world you will either understand and adapt to find success or you will fail

Now you can see how we make suboptimal decisions and repeat mistakes. We are afraid to learn and admit when we don't know enough. This is the mindset that leads to poor decisions. They are a source of stress and anxiety, and consume massive amounts of time. Not when we're making them—no, when we're making them they seem natural because they align with our view of how we want things to work. We get tripped up when the world doesn't work the way we want it to or when we fail to see what is. Rather than update our views, we double down our effort, accelerating our frustrations and anxiety. It's only weeks or months later, when we're spending massive amounts of time fixing our mistakes, that they start to increase their burden on us. Then we wonder why we have no time for family and friends and why we're so consumed by things outside of our control.

We are passive, thinking these things just happened to us and not that we did something to cause them. This passivity means that we rarely reflect on our decisions and the outcomes. Without reflection we cannot learn. Without learning we are doomed to repeat mistakes, become frustrated when the world doesn't work the way we want it to, and wonder why we are so busy. The cycle goes on.

But we are not passive participants in our decisions. The world does not act on us as much as it reveals itself to us and we respond. Ego gets in the way, locking reality behind a door that it controls with a gating mechanism. Only through persistence in the face of having it slammed on us over and over can we begin to see the light on the other side.

Ego, of course, is more than the enemy. It's also our friend. If we had a perfect view of the world and made decisions rationally, we would never attempt to do the amazing things that make us human. Ego propels us. Why, without ego, would we even attempt to travel to Mars? After all, it's never been done before. We'd never start a business because most of them fail. We need to learn to understand when ego serves us and when it hinders us. Wrapping ego up in outcomes instead of in ourselves makes it easier to update our views.

We optimize for short-term ego protection over long-term happiness. Increasingly, our understanding of things becomes black and white rather than shades of grey. When things happen in accord with our view of the world we naturally think they are good for us and others. When they conflict with

Despite having consistently bad results for patients,
bloodletting was practiced for over 2,000 years.

our views, they are wrong and bad. But the world is smarter than we are and it will teach us all we need to know if we're open to its feedback—if we keep our feet on the ground.

Mental models and how to use them

Perhaps an example will help illustrate the mental models approach. Think of gravity, something we learned about as kids and perhaps studied more formally in university as adults. We each have a mental model about gravity, whether we know it or not. And that model helps us to understand how gravity works. Of course we don't need to know all of the details, but we know what's important. We know, for instance, that if we drop a pen it will fall to the floor. If we see a pen on the floor we come to a probabilistic conclusion that gravity played a role.

This model plays a fundamental role in our lives. It explains the movement of the Earth around the sun. It informs the design of bridges and airplanes. It's one of the models we use to evaluate the safety of leaning on a guard rail or repairing a roof. But we also apply our understanding of gravity in other, less obvious ways. We use the model as a metaphor to explain the influence of strong personalities, as when we say, "He was pulled into her orbit." This is a reference to our basic understanding of the role of mass in gravity—the more there is the stronger the pull. It also informs some classic sales techniques. Gravity diminishes with distance, and so too does your propensity to make an impulse buy. Good salespeople know that the more distance you get, in time or geography, between yourself and the object of desire, the less likely you are to buy. Salespeople try to keep the pressure on to get you to buy right away.

Gravity has been around since before humans, so we can consider it to be time-tested, reliable, and representing reality. And yet, can you explain gravity with a ton of detail? I highly doubt it. And you don't need to for the model to be useful to you. Our understanding of gravity, in other words, our mental model, lets us anticipate what will happen and also helps us explain what has happened. We don't need to be able to describe the physics in detail for the model to be useful.

However, not every model is as reliable as gravity, and all models are flawed in some way. Some are reliable in some situations but useless in others. Some are too limited in their scope to be of much use. Others are unreliable because they haven't been tested and challenged, and yet others are just plain wrong. In every situation, we need to figure out which models are reliable and useful. We must also discard or update the unreliable ones, because unreliable or flawed models come with a cost.

For a long time people believed that bloodletting cured many different illnesses. This mistaken belief actually led doctors to contribute to the deaths of many of their patients. When we use flawed models we are more likely to misunderstand the situation, the variables that matter, and the cause and effect relationships between them. Because of such misunderstandings we often take suboptimal actions, like draining so much blood out of patients that they die from it.

Better models mean better thinking. The degree to which our models accurately explain reality is the degree to which they improve our thinking. Understanding reality is the name of the game. Understanding not only helps us decide which actions to take but helps us remove or avoid actions that have a big downside that we would otherwise not be aware of. Not only do we understand the immediate problem with more accuracy, but we can begin to see the second-, third-, and higher-order consequences. This understanding helps us eliminate avoidable errors. Sometimes making good decisions boils down to avoiding bad ones.

Flawed models, regardless of intentions, cause harm when they are put to use. When it comes to applying mental models we tend to run into trouble either when our model of

reality is wrong, that is, it doesn't survive real world experience, or when our model is right and we apply it to a situation
where it doesn't belong.

Models that don't hold up to reality cause massive
mistakes. Consider that the model of bloodletting as a cure
for disease caused unnecessary death because it weakened
patients when they needed all their strength to fight their
illnesses. It hung around for such a long time because it was
part of a package of flawed models, such as those explaining
the causes of sickness and how the human body worked, that
made it difficult to determine exactly where it didn't fit with
reality.

We compound the problem of flawed models when we
fail to update our models when evidence indicates they are
wrong. Only by repeated testing of our models against reality
and being open to feedback can we update our understanding
of the world and change our thinking. We need to look at the
results of applying the model over the largest sample size possible to be able to refine it so that it aligns with how the world
actually works.

— Sidebar: What Can the Three Buckets of Knowledge Teach Us About History?

The power of acquiring new models

The quality of our thinking is largely influenced by the mental
models in our heads. While we want accurate models, we also
want a wide variety of models to uncover what's really happening. The key here is variety. Most of us study something specific
and don't get exposure to the big ideas of other disciplines. We
don't develop the multidisciplinary mindset that we need to
accurately see a problem. And because we don't have the right
models to understand the situation, we overuse the models we
do have and use them even when they don't belong.

You've likely experienced this first hand. An engineer will
often think in terms of systems by default. A psychologist will

What Can the Three Buckets of Knowledge Teach Us About History?

"Every statistician knows that a large, relevant sample size is their best friend. What are the three largest, most relevant sample sizes for identifying universal principles? Bucket number one is inorganic systems, which are 13.7 billion years in size. It's all the laws of math and physics, the entire physical universe. Bucket number two is organic systems, 3.5 billion years of biology on Earth. And bucket number three is human history, you can pick your own number, I picked 20,000 years of recorded human behavior. Those are the three largest sample sizes we can access and the most relevant." —Peter Kaufman

The larger and more relevant the sample size, the more reliable the model based on it is. But the key to sample sizes is to look for them not just over space, but over time. You need to reach back into the past as far as you can to contribute to your sample. We have a tendency to think that how the world is, is how it always was. And so we get caught up validating our assumptions from what we find in the here and now. But the continents used to be pushed against each other, dinosaurs walked the planet for millions of years, and we are not the only hominid to evolve. Looking to the past can provide essential context for understanding where we are now.

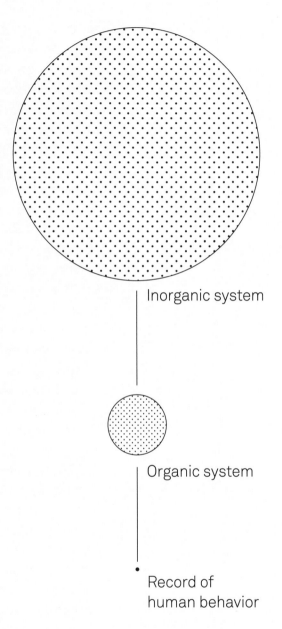

Inorganic system

Organic system

Record of
human behavior

1
Schlender, Brent.
"The Bill and Warren Show."
Fortune, July 20, 1998.
Retrieved from: http://archive.fortune.com/magazines/fortune/fortune_archive/1998/07/20/245683/index.html

think in terms of incentives. A business person might think in terms of opportunity cost and risk-reward. Through their disciplines, each of these people sees part of the situation, the part of the world that makes sense to them. None of them, however, see the entire situation unless they are thinking in a multidisciplinary way. In short, they have blind spots. Big blind spots. And they're not aware of their blind spots. There is an old adage that encapsulates this: "To the man with only a hammer, everything starts looking like a nail." Not every problem is a nail. The world is full of complications and interconnections that can only be explained through understanding of multiple models.

Removing blind spots means thinking through the problem using different lenses or models. When we do this the blind spots slowly go away and we gain an understanding of the problem.

We're much like the blind men in the classic parable of the elephant, going through life trying to explain everything through one limited lens. Too often that lens is driven by our particular field, be it economics, engineering, physics, mathematics, biology, chemistry, or something else entirely. Each of these disciplines holds some truth and yet none of them contain the whole truth.

Here's another way to look at it: think of a forest. When a botanist looks at it they may focus on the ecosystem, an environmentalist sees the impact of climate change, a forestry engineer the state of the tree growth, a business person the value of the land. None are wrong, but neither are any of them able to describe the full scope of the forest. Sharing knowledge, or learning the basics of the other disciplines, would lead to a more well-rounded understanding that would allow for better initial decisions about managing the forest.

Relying on only a few models is like having a 400-horsepower brain that's only generating 50 horsepower of output. To increase your mental efficiency and reach your

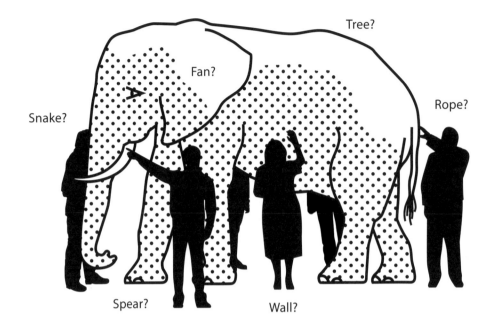

A group of blind people approach a strange animal, called an elephant. None of them are aware of its shape and form. So they decide to understand it by touch. The first person, whose hand touches the trunk, says, "This creature is like a thick snake." For the second person, whose hand finds an ear, it seems like a type of fan. The third person, whose hand is on a leg, says the elephant is a pillar like a tree-trunk. The fourth blind man who places his hand on the side says, "An elephant is a wall." The fifth, who feels its tail, describes it as a rope. The last touches its tusk, and states the elephant is something that is hard and smooth, like a spear.

1
Munger, Charlie.
"A Lesson on Elementary, Worldly
Wisdom As It Relates to Investment
Management & Business." Lecture
to USC Business School, 1994.
Retrieved from: https://old.ycombi-
nator.com/munger.html

2
De Botton, Alain, and Diyala Muir.
"How To Make a Decision."
The School of Life production.
Retrieved from: https://youtu.be/
okdsAZUTJ94

400-horsepower potential, you need to use a latticework of mental models. Exactly the same sort of pattern that graces backyards everywhere, a lattice is a series of points that connect to and reinforce each other. The Great Models can be understood in the same way—models influence and interact with each other to create a structure that can be used to evaluate and understand ideas.

In a famous speech in the 1990s, Charlie Munger summed up this approach to practical wisdom: "Well, the first rule is that you can't really know anything if you just remember isolated facts and try and bang 'em back. If the facts don't hang together on a latticework of theory, you don't have them in a usable form. You've got to have models in your head. And you've got to array your experience both vicarious and direct on this latticework of models. You may have noticed students who just try to remember and pound back what is remembered. Well, they fail in school and in life. You've got to hang experience on a latticework of models in your head."[1]

«The chief enemy of good decisions is a lack of sufficient perspectives on a problem.»

Alain de Botton[2]

Expanding your latticework of mental models

A latticework is an excellent way to conceptualize mental models, because it demonstrates the reality and value of interconnecting knowledge. The world does not isolate itself into discrete disciplines. We only break it down that way because it makes it easier to study it. But once we learn something, we need to put it back into the complex system in which it occurs. We need to see where it connects to other bits of knowledge, to build our understanding of the whole. This is the value of putting the knowledge contained in mental models into a latticework.

It reduces the blind spots that limit our view of not only the immediate problem, but the second and subsequent order effects of our potential solutions. Without a latticework of the Great Models our decisions become harder, slower, and less creative. But by using a mental models approach, we can complement our specializations by being curious about how the rest of the world works. A quick glance at the Nobel Prize winners list show that many of them, obviously extreme specialists in something, had multidisciplinary interests that supported their achievements.

To help you build your latticework of mental models, this book, and the books that follow, attempt to arm you with the big models from multiple disciplines. We'll take a look at biology, physics, chemistry, economics, and even psychology. We don't need to master all the details from these disciplines, just the fundamentals.

To quote Charlie Munger, "80 or 90 important models will carry about 90 percent of the freight in making you a worldly-wise person. And, of those, only a mere handful really carry very heavy freight." [1]

These books attempt to collect and make accessible organized common sense—the 80 to 90 mental models you need to get started. To help you understand the models, we will relate them to historical examples and stories. Our website **fs.blog** will have even more practical examples.

The more high-quality mental models you have in your mental toolbox, the more likely you will have the ones needed to understand the problem. And understanding is everything. The better you understand, the better the potential actions you can take. The better the potential actions, the fewer problems you'll encounter down the road. Better models make better decisions.

1
Munger, Charles.
Poor Charlie's Almanack.
Peter D. Kaufman ed. Missouri:
Walsworth Publishing Company,
2005.

1
Munger, Charlie.
Ibid.

« I think it is undeniably true that the
human brain must work in models.
The trick is to have your brain work better
than the other person's brain because it
understands the most fundamental models:
ones that will do most work per unit.
If you get into the mental habit of relating
what you're reading to the basic structure of
the underlying ideas being demonstrated,
you gradually accumulate some wisdom. »

Charlie Munger [1]

It takes time, but the benefits are enormous

What successful people do is file away a massive, but finite,
amount of fundamental, established, essentially unchanging
knowledge that can be used in evaluating the infinite number
of unique scenarios which show up in the real world.

It's not just knowing the mental models that is important. First you must learn them, but then you must use them.
Each decision presents an opportunity to comb through your
repertoire and try one out, so you can also learn how to use
them. This will slow you down at first, and you won't always
choose the right models, but you will get better and more
efficient at using mental models as time progresses.

We need to work hard at synthesizing across the borders
of our knowledge, and most importantly, synthesizing all of the
ideas we learn with *reality itself*. No model contains the entire
truth, whatever that may be. What good are math and biology
and psychology unless we know how they fit together in reality
itself, and how to use them to make our lives better? It would
be like dying of hunger because we don't know how to combine
and cook any of the foods in our pantry.

1
Simon, Herbert A.
Models of My Life.
Cambridge: MIT Press, 1996

« Disciplines, like nations, are a necessary evil that enable human beings of bounded rationality to simplify their goals and reduce their choices to calculable limits. But parochialism is everywhere, and the world badly needs international and interdisciplinary travelers to carry new knowledge from one enclave to another.»

Herbert Simon [1]

You won't always get it right. Sometimes the model, or models, you choose to use won't be the best ones for that situation. That's okay. The more you use them, the more you will be able to build the knowledge of indicators that can trigger the use of the most appropriate model. Using and failing, as long as you acknowledge, reflect, and learn from it, is also how you build your repertoire.

You need to be deliberate about choosing the models you will use in a situation. As you use them, a great practice is to record and reflect. That way you can get better at both choosing models and applying them. Take the time to notice how you applied them, what the process was like, and what the results were. Over time you will develop your knowledge of which situations are best tackled through which models. Don't give up on a model if it doesn't help you right away. Learn more about it, and try to figure out exactly why it didn't work. It may be that you have to improve your understanding. Or that there were aspects of the situation that you did not consider. Or that your focus was on the wrong variable. So keep a journal. Write your experiences down. When you identify a model at work in the world, write that down too. Then you can explore the applications you've observed, and start being more in control of the models you use every day. For instance, instead of falling victim to confirmation bias, you will be able to step back and see it at work in yourself and others. Once you get practice, you will start to naturally apply models as you go through your life, from reading the news to contemplating a career move.

As we have seen, we can run into problems when we apply models to situations in which they don't fit. If a model works, we must invest the time and energy into understanding why it worked so we know when to use it again. At the beginning the process is more important than the outcome. As you use the models, stay open to the feedback loops. Reflect and learn. You will get better. It will become easier. Results will become more profoundly useful, more broadly applicable, and more memorable. While this book isn't intended to be a book specifically about making better decisions, it will help you make better decisions. Mental models are not an excuse to create a lengthy decision process but rather to help you move away from seeing things the way you think they should be to the way they are. Uncovering this knowledge will naturally help your decision-making. Right now you are only touching one part of the elephant, so you are making all decisions based on your understanding that it's a wall or a rope, not an animal. As soon as you begin to take in the knowledge that other people have of the world, like learning the perspectives others have of the elephant, you will start having more success because your decisions will be aligned with how the world really is.

When you start to understand the world better, when the whys seem less mysterious, you gain confidence in how you navigate it. The successes will accrue. And more success means more time, less stress, and ultimately a more meaningful life.

Time to dive in.

The Map is not the Territory

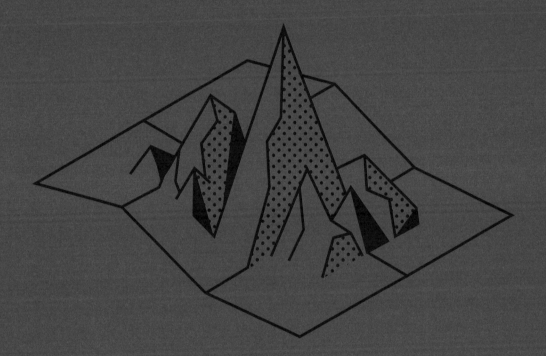

Reality check.

The map appears
to us more real than
the land.

D.H. Lawrence[1]

The Map is not the Territory

The map of reality is not reality. Even the best maps are imperfect. That's because they are reductions of what they represent. If a map were to represent the territory with perfect fidelity, it would no longer be a reduction and thus would no longer be useful to us. A map can also be a snapshot of a point in time, representing something that no longer exists. This is important to keep in mind as we think through problems and make better decisions.

We use maps every day. They help us navigate from one city to another. They help us reduce complexity to simplicity. Think of the financial statements for a company, which are meant to distill the complexity of thousands of transactions into something simpler. Or a policy document on office procedure, a manual on parenting a two-year-old, or your performance review. All are models or maps that simplify some complex territory in order to guide you through it.

Just because maps and models are flawed is not an excuse to ignore them. Maps are useful to the extent they are explanatory and predictive.

Key elements of a map

In 1931, the mathematician Alfred Korzybski[*] presented a paper on mathematical semantics in New Orleans, Louisiana. Looking at it today, most of the paper reads like a complex, technical argument on the relationship of mathematics to human language, and of both to physical reality.

However, with this paper Korzybski introduced and popularized the concept that *the map is not the territory.* In other words, the description of the thing is not the thing itself. The model is not reality. The abstraction is not the abstracted. Specifically, in his own words:[2]

1
Lawrence, D.H.
Study of Thomas Hardy. Phoenix: The Posthumous Papers of D.H. Lawrence, Edward McDonald, ed. London: William Heinemann, 1936.

*
Korzybski, Alfred.
1879-1950 - Polish-American independent scholar who developed the field of general semantics. He argued that knowledge is limited by our physical and language capabilities.

2
Korzybski, Alfred.
Science and Sanity.
New York: Institute of General Semantics, 1933.

1.

A map may have a structure similar or dissimilar to the structure of the territory. The London underground map is super useful to travelers. The train drivers don't use it at all! Maps describe a territory in a useful way, but with a specific purpose. They cannot be everything to everyone.

2.

Two similar structures have similar "logical" characteristics. If a correct map shows Dresden as between Paris and Warsaw, a similar relation is found in the actual territory. If you have a map showing where Dresden is, you should be able to use it to get there.

3.

A map is not the actual territory. The London underground map does not convey what it's like to be standing in Covent Garden station. Nor would you use it to navigate out of the station.

4.

An ideal map would contain the map of the map, the map of the map of the map, etc., endlessly. We may call this characteristic self-reflexiveness. Imagine using an overly complicated "Guide to Paris" on a trip to France, and then having to purchase another book that was the "Guide to the Guide of Paris". And so on. Ideally, you'd never have any issues—but eventually, the level of detail would be overwhelming.

The truth is, the only way we can navigate the complexity of reality is through some sort of abstraction. When we read the news, we're consuming abstractions created by other people. The authors consumed vast amounts of information, reflected upon it, and drew some abstractions and conclusions that they share with us. But something is lost in the process. We can lose

Newton, Sir Isaac.
1643-1727 - English polymath. One
of the most influential scientists
of all time. He related the workings
of the Earth to the wonders of the
universe. He also spent 27 years
being Master of the Royal Mint.

the specific and relevant details that were distilled into an abstraction. And, because we often consume these abstractions as gospel, without having done the hard mental work ourselves, it's tricky to see when the map no longer agrees with the territory. We inadvertently forget that the map is not reality.

But my GPS didn't show that cliff

We need maps and models as guides. But frequently, we don't remember that our maps and models are abstractions and thus we fail to understand their limits. We forget there is a territory that exists separately from the map. This territory contains details the map doesn't describe. We run into problems when our knowledge becomes of the *map*, rather than the actual underlying territory it describes.

When we mistake the map for reality, we start to think we have all the answers. We create static rules or policies that deal with the map but forget that we exist in a constantly changing world. When we close off or ignore feedback loops, we don't see the terrain has changed and we dramatically reduce our ability to adapt to a changing environment. Reality is messy and complicated, so our tendency to simplify it is understandable. However, if the aim becomes simplification rather than understanding we start to make bad decisions.

We can't use maps as dogma. Maps and models are not meant to live forever as static references. The world is dynamic. As territories change, our tools to navigate them must be flexible to handle a wide variety of situations or adapt to the changing times. If the value of a map or model is related to its ability to predict or explain, then it needs to represent reality. If reality has changed the map must change.

Take Newtonian[*] physics. For hundreds of years it served as an extremely useful model for understanding the workings of our world. From gravity to celestial motion, Newtonian physics was a wide-ranging map.

—

Would you be able to use this map to get to Egypt?

Einstein, Albert.
1879-1955 - German theoretical
physicist who gave us the theory
of relativity and opened up the
universe. He is famous for many
things, including his genius, his
kindness and his hair.

*
Ostrom, Elinor.
1933-2012 - American political
economist. In 2009 she shared
the Nobel Memorial Prize in
Economic Sciences for her analysis
of economic governance; in particular, questions related to "the
commons".

Then in 1905 Albert Einstein*, with his theory of Special Relativity, changed our understanding of the universe in a huge way. He replaced the understanding handed down by Isaac Newton hundreds of years earlier. He created a new map.

Newtonian physics is still a *very* useful model. One can use it very reliably to predict the movement of objects large and small, with some limitations as pointed out by Einstein. And, on the flip side, Einstein's physics are still not totally com- plete: With every year that goes by, physicists become increas- ingly frustrated with their inability to tie it into small-scale quantum physics. Another map may yet come.

But what physicists do so well, and most of us do so poorly, is that they carefully delimit what Newtonian and Ein- steinian physics are able to explain. They know down to many decimal places where those maps are useful guides to reality, and where they aren't. And when they hit uncharted territory, like quantum mechanics, they explore it carefully instead of assuming the maps they have can explain it all.

Maps can't show everything

Some of the biggest map/territory problems are the risks of the *territory* that are not shown on the *map*. When we're following the map without looking around, we trip right over them. Any user of a map or model must realize that we do not understand a model, map, or reduction unless we understand and respect its limitations. If we don't understand what the map does and doesn't tell us, it can be useless or even dangerous.

— Sidebar: The Tragedy of the Commons

Here's another way to think about it. Economist Elinor Ostrom* wrote about being cautious with maps and models when look- ing at different governance structures for common resources. She was worried that the Tragedy of the Commons model (see sidebar), which shows how a shared resource can become destroyed through bad incentives, was too general and did

The Tragedy of the Commons

The Tragedy of the Commons is a parable that illustrates why common resources get used more than is desirable from the standpoint of society as a whole. Garrett Hardin wrote extensively about this concept.

"Picture a pasture open to all. It is to be expected that each herdsman will try to keep as many cattle as possible on the commons. Such an arrangement may work reasonably satisfactorily for centuries because tribal wars, poaching, and disease keep the numbers of both man and beast well below the carrying capacity of the land. Finally, however, comes the day of reckoning, that is, the day when the long-desired goal of social stability becomes a reality. At this point, the inherent logic of the commons remorselessly generates tragedy.

As a rational being, each herdsman seeks to maximize his gain. Explicitly or implicitly, more or less consciously, he asks, "What is the utility to me of adding one more animal to my herd?" This utility has one negative and one positive component.

1. The positive component is a function of the increment of one animal. Since the herdsman receives all the proceeds from the sale of the additional animal, the positive utility is nearly +1.

2. The negative component is a function of the additional overgrazing created by one more animal. Since, however, the effects of overgrazing are shared by all the herdsmen, the negative utility for any particular decision-making herdsman is only a fraction of 1.

Adding together the component partial utilities, the rational herdsman concludes that the only sensible course for him to pursue is to add another animal to his herd. And another; and another.... But this is the conclusion reached by each and every rational herdsman sharing a commons. Therein is the tragedy.

Each man is locked into a system that compels him to increase his herd without limit—in a world that is limited. Ruin is the destination toward which all men rush, each pursuing his own best interest in a society that believes in the freedom of the commons. Freedom in a commons brings ruin to all." [1]

What is common to many is taken least care of, for all men have greater regard for what is their own than for what they possess in common with others. –Aristotle

[1]
Hardin, Garrett.
The Tragedy of the Commons,
Science, 13 December 1968, vol. 162, pp. 1243-48

1
Ostrom, Elinor.
*Governing the Commons: The Evo-
lution of Institutions for Collective
Action.* UK: Cambridge University
Press, 1990.

2
Box, George E P.
Ibid.

not account for how people, in reality, solved the problem. She explained the limitations of using models to guide public policy, namely that they often become metaphors.

> *"What makes these models so dangerous … is that the constraints that are assumed to be fixed for the purpose of analysis are taken on faith as being fixed in empirical setting."*[1]

This is a double problem. First, having a general map, we may assume that if a territory matches the map in a couple of respects it matches the map in all respects. Second, we may think adherence to the map is more important than taking in new information about a territory. Ostrom asserts that one of the main values of using models as maps in public policy discussions is in the thinking that is generated. They are tools for exploration, not doctrines to force conformity. They are guidebooks, not laws.

« Remember that all models are wrong; the practical question is how wrong do they have to be to not be useful. »

George Box[2]

In order to use a map or model as accurately as possible, we should take three important considerations into account:

1. **Reality is the ultimate update.**
2. **Consider the cartographer.**
3. **Maps can influence territories.**

Reality is the ultimate update: When we enter new and unfamiliar territory it's nice to have a map on hand. Everything from travelling to a new city, to becoming a parent for the first time has maps that we can use to improve our ability to navigate the terrain. But territories change, sometimes faster than the maps and models that describe them. We can and should update them based on our own experiences in the territory. That's how good maps are built: feedback loops created by explorers.

We can think of stereotypes as maps. Sometimes they are useful—we have to process large amounts of information every day, and simplified chunks such as stereotypes can help us sort through this information with efficiency. The danger is when, like with all maps, we forget the territory is more complex. That people have far more territory than a stereotype can represent.

In the early 1900s, Europeans were snapping pictures all over Palestine, leaving a record that may have reflected their ethnographic perspective, but did not cover Karimeh Abbud's[*] perception of her culture. She began to take photos of those around her, becoming the first female Arab to set up her own photo studio in Palestine. Her pictures reflected a different take on the territory—she rejected the European style and aimed to capture the middle class as they were. She tried to let her camera record the territory as she saw it versus manipulating the images to follow a narrative.

Her informal style and desire to photograph the variety around her, from landscapes to intimate portraits, have left a legacy far beyond the photos themselves.[1,2] She contributed a different perspective, a new map, with which to explore the history of the territory of Palestine.

We do have to remember though, that a map captures a territory at a moment in time. Just because it might have done a good job at depicting what was, there is no guarantee that it depicts what is there now or what will be there in the future. The faster the rate of change in the territory, the harder it will be for a map to keep up to date.

[*]
Abbud, Karimeh.
1893-1955 - Palestinian professional photographer. Also known as the "Lady Photographer", she was an artist who lived and worked in Lebanon and Palestine.

[1]
Nassar, Issam.
Early Local Photography in Palestine: The Legacy of Karimeh Abbud. Jerusalem Quarterly. Issue 46, Summer 2011.

[2]
Mrowat, Ahmed.
Karimeh Abbud: Early Woman Photographer. Jerusalem Quarterly. Issue 31, Summer 2007.

—

Dividing a large chunk of the Middle East into simply A and
B, the Sykes-Picot line proposed borders that paid little
regard to ethnic or geographical features.

« Viewed in its development through time, the map details the changing thought of the human race, and few works seem to be such an excellent indicator of culture and civilization. »

Norman J.W. Thrower[1]

1
Thrower, Norman J.W.
Maps and Civilization: Cartography in Culture and Society. Chicago: University of Chicago Press, 1999.

2
MacMillan, Margaret.
The Uses and Abuses of History. Toronto: Penguin, 2008.

3
An excellent analysis of the division of the Middle East after World War I can be found in: MacMillan, Margaret. *Paris 1919: Six Months that Changed the World.* New York: Random House, 2001.

Consider the cartographer: Maps are not purely objective creations. They reflect the values, standards, and limitations of their creators. We can see this in the changing national boundaries that make up our world maps. Countries come and go depending on shifting political and cultural sensibilities. When we look at the world map we have today, we tend to associate societies with nations, assuming that the borders reflect a common identity shared by everyone contained within them.

However, as historian Margaret MacMillan has pointed out, nationalism is a very modern construct, and in some sense has developed with, not in advance of, the maps that set out the shape of countries.[2] We then should not assume that our literal maps depict an objective view of the geographical territory. For example, historians have shown that the modern borders of Syria, Jordan, and Iraq reflect British and French determination to maintain influence in the Middle East after World War I.[3] Thus, they are a better map of Western interest than of local custom and organization. Models, then, are most useful when we consider them in the context they were created. What was the cartographer trying to achieve? How does this influence what is depicted in the map?

Jacobs, Jane.
1916-2006 - American-Canadian
journalist, author, and activist who
influenced urban studies, sociol-
ogy, and economics. Her work has
greatly impacted the development
of North American cities.

1
Thrower, Norman J.W.
Ibid.

2
Jacobs, Jane.
*The Death and Life of Great
American Cities*. New York: Vintage
Books, 1992. (Original published
1961). Page 438.

« As a branch of human endeavor,
cartography has a long and interesting
history that well reflects the state of
cultural activity, as well as the perception
of the world, in different periods. …
Though technical in nature, cartography,
like architecture, has attributes of both
a scientific and artistic pursuit,
a dichotomy not satisfactorily reconciled
in all presentations. »

Norman J.W. Thrower[1]

Maps can influence territories: This problem was part of the central argument put forth by Jane Jacobs* in her ground-breaking work, *The Death and Life of Great American Cities*. She chronicled the efforts of city planners who came up with elaborate models for the design and organization of cities without paying any attention to how cities actually work. They then tried to fit the cities into the model. She describes how cities were changed to correspond to these models, and the often negative consequences of these efforts. "It became pos-sible also to map out master plans for the statistical city, and people take these more seriously, for we are all accustomed to believe that maps and reality are necessarily related, or that if they are not, we can make them so by altering reality." [2]

Jacobs' book is, in part, a cautionary tale of what can happen when faith in the model influences the decisions we make in the territory. When we try to fit complexity into the simplification.

Jacobs demonstrated that mapping the interaction between people and sidewalks was an important factor in determining how to improve city safety.

1
Hand, David J.
*Wonderful Examples, but Let's
not Close Our Eyes.* Statist.
Sci. 29 (2014), no. 1, 98--100.
doi:10.1214/13-STS446

« In general, when building statistical models, we must not forget that the aim is to understand something about the real world. Or predict, choose an action, make a decision, summarize evidence, and so on, but always about the real world, not an abstract mathematical world: our models are not the reality. »

David Hand [1]

Conclusion

Maps have long been a part of human society. They are valuable tools to pass on knowledge. Still, in using maps, abstractions, and models, we must always be wise to their limitations. They are, by definition, reductions of something far more complex. There is always at least an element of subjectivity, and we need to remember that they are created at particular moments in time.

This does not mean that we cannot use maps and models. We must use some model of the world in order to simplify it and therefore interact with it. We cannot explore every bit of territory for ourselves. We can use maps to guide us, but we must not let them prevent us from discovering new territory or updating our existing maps.

While navigating the world based on terrain is a useful goal, it's not always possible. Maps, and models, help us understand and relate to the world around us. They are flawed but useful. In order to think a few steps ahead we must think beyond the map.

Model of Management

Let's take a model of management. There are hundreds of them, dating back at least to the Scientific Theory of Management by Frederick Taylor, which had factory managers breaking down tasks into small pieces, forcing their workers to specialize, and financially incentivizing them to complete those tasks efficiently. It was a brute force method, but it worked pretty well.

As time went on and the economy increasingly moved away from manufacturing, other theories gained popularity, and Taylor's scientific model is no longer used by anyone of note. That does not mean it wasn't useful: For a time, it was. It's just that reality is more complicated than Taylor's model. It had to contend with at least the following factors:

1. As more and more people know what model you're using to manipulate them, they may decide not to respond to your incentives.

2. As your competitors gain knowledge of the model, they respond in kind by adopting the model themselves, thus flattening the field.

3. The model may have been mostly useful in a factory setting, and not in an office setting, or a technology setting.

4. Human beings are not simple automatons: A more complete model would hone in on other motivations they might have besides financial ones.

And so on. Clearly, though Taylor's model was effective for a time, it was effective with limitations. As with Einstein eclipsing Newton, better models came along in time.

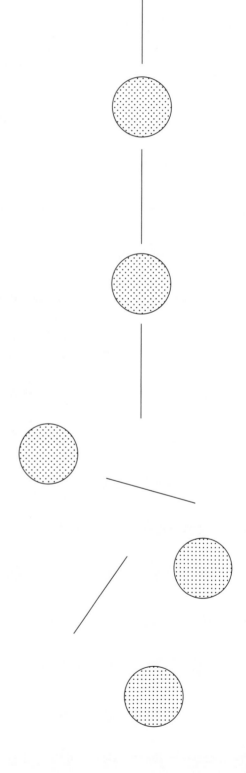

Maps Are Necessarily Flawed

Maps, or models, are necessary but necessarily flawed. Lewis Carroll once jabbed at this in a story called *Sylvie and Bruno*, where one of the characters decided that his country would create a map with the scale of one mile to one mile. Obviously, such a map would not have the limitations of a map, but it wouldn't be of much help either. You couldn't use it to actually go anywhere. It wouldn't fit in your pocket or your car. We need maps to condense the territory we are trying to navigate.

—
Illustration from the first edition of *Sylvie and Bruno*, published in 1889

Circle of Competence

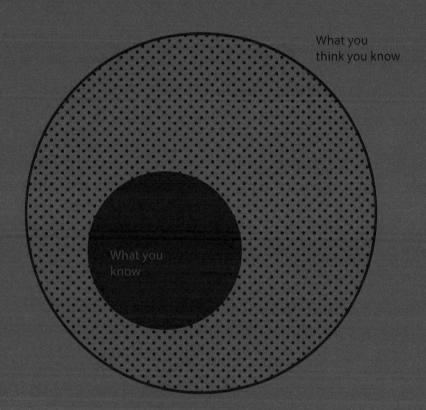

What you
think you know

What you
know

—
What don't you know?

I'm no genius. I'm smart in spots—but I stay around those spots.

Thomas Watson[1]

Circle of Competence

When ego and not competence drives what we undertake, we have blind spots. If you know what you understand, you know where you have an edge over others. When you are honest about where your knowledge is lacking you know where you are vulnerable and where you can improve. Understanding your circle of competence improves decision-making and outcomes.

In order to get the most out of this mental model, we will explore the following:

1. What is a circle of competence?
2. How do you know when you have one?
3. How do you build and maintain one?
4. How do you operate outside of one?

What is a circle of competence? Imagine an old man who's spent his entire life up in a small town. He's the Lifer. No detail of the goings-on in the town has escaped his notice over the years. He knows the lineage, behavior, attitudes, jobs, income, and social status of every person in town. Bit by bit, he built that knowledge up over a long period of observation and participation in town affairs.

The Lifer knows where the bodies are buried and who buried them. He knows who owes money to whom, who gets along with whom, and who the town depends on to keep spinning. He knows about that time the mayor cheated on his taxes. He knows about that time the town flooded, how many inches high the water was, and exactly who helped whom and who didn't.

Now imagine a Stranger enters the town, in from the Big City. Within a few days, the Stranger decides that he knows all there is to know about the town. He's met the mayor, the sheriff, the bartender, and the shopkeeper, and he can get around fairly easily. It's a small town and he hasn't come across anything surprising.

1
Watson, Thomas J., and Peter Petrie. *Father, Son, & Co.: My Life at IBM and Beyond.* New York: Random House, 2013.

In the Stranger's mind, he's convinced he pretty much knows everything a Lifer would know. He has sized up the town in no time, with his keen eye. He makes assumptions based on what he has learned so far, and figures he knows enough to get his business done. This, however, is a false sense of confidence that likely causes him to take more risks than he realizes. Without intimately knowing the history of the town, how can he be sure that he has picked the right land for development, or negotiated the best price?

After all, what kind of knowledge does he really have, compared to the Lifer?

The difference between the detailed web of knowledge in the Lifer's head and the surface knowledge in the Stranger's head is the difference between being inside a circle of competence and being outside the perimeter. True knowledge of a complex territory cannot be faked. The Lifer could stump the Stranger in no time, but not the other way around. Consequently, as long as the Lifer is operating in his circle of competence he will always have a better understanding of reality to use in making decisions. Having this deep knowledge gives him flexibility in responding to challenges, because he will likely have more than one solution to every problem. And this depth increases his efficiency—he can eliminate bad choices quickly because he has all the pieces of the puzzle.

What happens when you take the Lifer/Stranger idea seriously and try to delineate carefully the domains in which you're one or the other? There is no definite checklist for figuring this out, but if you don't have at least a few years and a few failures under your belt, you cannot consider yourself competent in a circle.

Norgay, Tenzing, born Namgyal
Wangdi. 1914-1986 - Nepali Sherpa
mountaineer. *Time* named him one
of the 100 most influential people of
the 20th century.

1
Sun Tzu.
The Art of War: With Study Guide.
New York: Hachette Book Group,
2015.

2
Pierce, Robert.
"Tenzing Norgay Sherpa." From
Tenzing Norgay Adventures website.
Retrieved from: http://www.ten-
zing-norgay.com/pages/tenzing-
norgaysherpa.html

3
Roberts, David.
"Everest 1953: First Footsteps -
Sir Edmund Hillary and Tenzing
Norgay." NationalGeographic.com.
Retrieved from: https://www.na-
tionalgeographic.com/adventure/
features/everest/sir-edmund-hil-
lary-tenzing-norgay-1953/

4
Schaffer, Grayson.
"The Disposable Man: A Western
History of Sherpas on Everest."
Outside Online, July 10, 2013.
Retrieved from: https://www.
outsideonline.com/1928326/
disposable-man-western-histo-
ry-sherpas-everest

« We shall be unable to turn natural advantage to account unless we make use of local guides. »

Sun Tzu [1]

For most of us, climbing to the summit of Mount Everest is outside our circles of competence. Not only do we have no real idea how to do it, but—even more scary—should we attempt it, we don't even know what we don't know. If we studied hard, maybe we'd figure out the basics. We'd learn about the training, the gear, the process, the time of year, all the things an outsider could quickly know. But at what point would you be satisfied that you knew enough to get up there, and back, with your life intact? And how confident would you be in this assessment?

There are approximately 200 bodies on Everest (not to mention the ones that have been removed). All of those people thought they could get up and down alive. The climate pre-serves their corpses, almost as a warning. The ascent to the summit takes you by the bodies of people who once shared your dreams.

Since the first recorded attempts to climb Everest in 1922, all climbers have relied on the specialized knowledge of the Sherpa people to help navigate the terrain of the mountain. Indigenous to the region, Sherpas grew up in the shadows of the mountain, uniquely placed to develop the circle of compe-tence necessary to get to the top.

Sherpa Tenzing Norgay* led the team that made the first ascent [2], and a quarter of all subsequent ascents have been made by Sherpas (some going as many as 16 times). [3,4] Although the mountain is equally risky for everyone, most people who climb Everest do it once. For the Sherpas, working and climbing various parts of the mountain is their day job. Would you try to climb Everest without their help?

Sherpa Tenzing Norgay and his ilk are the real lifers.
Yet strangers often ignore their advice much to their peril.

The physical challenges alone of reaching the summit are staggering. It is a region that humans aren't suited for. There isn't enough oxygen in the air and the top is regularly pummeled by winds of more than 150 miles an hour—stronger than a Category 5 hurricane. You don't get to the top on a whim, and you don't survive with only luck. Norgay worked for years as a trekking porter, and was part of a team that tried to ascend Everest in 1935. He finally succeeded in reaching the summit in 1953, after 20 years of climbing and trekking in the region. He developed his expertise through lots of lucky failures. After Everest, Norgay opened a mountaineering school to train other locals as guides, and a trekking company to take others climbing in the Himalayas.

Norgay is around the closest someone could come to being a Lifer when it comes to the competence required to climb Mount Everest.

How do you know when you have a circle of competence?

Within our circles of competence, we know exactly what we **don't** know. We are able to make decisions quickly and relatively accurately. We possess detailed knowledge of additional information we might need to make a decision with full understanding, or even what information is unobtainable. We know what is knowable and what is unknowable and can distinguish between the two.

We can anticipate and respond to objections because we've heard them before and already put in the work of gaining the knowledge to counter them. We also have a lot of options when we confront problems in our circles. Our deep fluency in subjects we are dealing with means we can draw on different information resources and understand what can be adjusted and what is invariant.

A circle of competence cannot be built quickly. We don't become Lifers overnight. It isn't the result of taking a few courses or working at something for a few months—being a

Lifer requires more than skimming the surface. In Alexander Pope's poem "An Essay on Criticism," he writes:

> *"A little learning is a dangerous thing;*
> *Drink deep, or taste not the Pierian spring:*
> *There shallow draughts intoxicate the brain,*
> *And drinking largely sobers us again."* [1]

There is no shortcut to understanding. Building a circle of competence takes years of experience, of making mistakes, and of actively seeking out better methods of practice and thought.

How do you build and maintain a circle of competence?

One of the essential requirements of a circle of competence is that you can never take it for granted. You can't operate as if a circle of competence is a static thing, that once attained is attained for life. The world is dynamic. Knowledge gets updated, and so too must your circle.

There are three key practices needed in order to build and maintain a circle of competence: curiosity and a desire to learn, monitoring, and feedback.

First, you have to be willing to learn. Learning comes when experience meets reflection. You can learn from your own experiences. Or you can learn from the experience of others, through books, articles, and conversations. Learning everything on your own is costly and slow. You are one person. Learning from the experiences of others is much more productive. You need to always approach your circle with curiosity, seeking out information that can help you expand and strengthen it.

« Learn from the mistakes of others. You can't live long enough to make them all yourself. »

Anonymous

1
Pope, Alexander. "An Essay On Criticism." Poetry Foundation, n. d. Retrieved from: https://www.poetry-foundation.org/articles/69379/an-essay-on-criticism

Second, you need to monitor your track record in areas which you have, or want to have, a circle of competence. And you need to have the courage to monitor honestly so the feedback can be used to your advantage.

The reason we have such difficulty with overconfidence—as demonstrated in studies which show that most of us are much worse drivers, lovers, managers, traders (and many other things) than we think we are—is because we have a problem with honest self-reporting. We don't keep the right records, because we don't *really* want to know what we're good and bad at. Ego is a powerful enemy when it comes to better understanding reality.

But that won't work if you're trying to assess or build your circle of competence. You need to keep a precise diary of your trades, if you're investing in the stock market. If you are in a leadership position, you need to observe and chronicle the results of your decisions and evaluate them based on what you were trying to achieve. You need to be honest about your failures in order to reflect and learn from them. That's what it takes.

Keeping a journal of your own performance is the easiest and most private way to give self-feedback. Journals allow you to step out of your automatic thinking and ask yourself: What went wrong? How could I do better? Monitoring your own performance allows you to see patterns that you simply couldn't see before. This type of analysis is painful for the ego, which is also why it helps build a circle of competence. You can't improve if you don't know what you're doing wrong.

Finally, you must occasionally solicit external feedback. This helps build a circle, but is also critical for maintaining one.

A lot of professionals have an ego problem: their view of themselves does not line up with the way other people see them. Before people can change they need to know these outside views. We need to go to people we trust, who can give us honest feedback about our traits. These people are in a position to observe us operating within our circles, and are thus able to offer relevant perspectives on our competence. Another option is to hire a coach.

Atul Gawande[*] is one of the top surgeons in the United States. And when he wanted to get better at being a surgeon, he hired a coach. This is terribly difficult for anyone, let alone a doctor. At first he felt embarrassed. It had been over a decade since he was evaluated by another person in medical school. "Why," he asked, "should I expose myself to the scrutiny and fault-finding?"[1]

The coach worked. Gawande got two things out of this. First, Gawande received something he couldn't see himself and something no one else would point out (if they noticed it at all): knowledge of where his skill and technique was suboptimal. The second thing Gawande took away was the ability to provide better feedback to other doctors.

It is extremely difficult to maintain a circle of competence without an outside perspective. We usually have too many biases to solely rely on our own observations. It takes courage to solicit external feedback, so if defensiveness starts to manifest, focus on the result you hope to achieve.

How do you operate outside a circle of competence?

Part of successfully using circles of competence includes knowing when we are outside them—when we are not well equipped to make decisions. Since we can't be inside a circle of competence in everything, when we find ourselves Strangers in a place filled with Lifers, what do we do? We don't always get to "stay around our spots." We must develop a repertoire of techniques for managing when we're outside of our sphere, which happens all the time.[2]

[*]
Gawande, Atul.
1965 - American surgeon, writer, and public health researcher. He practices medicine in Boston, is a professor at Harvard University, and has been a staff writer for The New Yorker since 1998.

[1]
Gawande, Atul.
"Personal Best," The New Yorker, October 3, 2011. Retrieved from: https://www.newyorker.com/magazine/2011/10/03/personal-best (Accessed January 23, 2018)

[2]
Part of the Circle of Competence means that you know when you're not the best person to make the decision and you can allow someone else with a comparative advantage in this area to make the decision.

There are three parts to successfully operating outside a circle of competence:

1.   Learn at least the basics of the realm you're operating in, while acknowledging that you're a Stranger, not a Lifer. However, keep in mind that basic information is easy to obtain and often gives the acquirer an unwarranted confidence.

2.   Talk to someone whose circle of competence in the area is strong. Take the time to do a bit of research to at least define questions you need to ask, and what information you need, to make a good decision. If you ask a person to answer the question for you, they'll be giving you a fish. If you ask them detailed and thoughtful questions, you'll learn how to fish. Furthermore, when you need the advice of others, especially in higher stakes situations, ask questions to probe the limits of their circles. Then ask yourself how the situation might influence the information they choose to provide you.

3.   Use a broad understanding of the basic mental models of the world to augment your limited understanding of the field in which you find yourself a Stranger. These will help you identify the foundational concepts that would be most useful. These then serve as a guide to help you navigate the situation you are in.

There are inevitably areas where you are going to be a Stranger, even in the profession in which you excel. It is impossible for our circles of competence to encompass the entire world. Even if we're careful to know the boundaries and take them seriously, we can't always operate inside our circles. Life is simply not that forgiving. We have to make HR decisions without being

The Problem of Incentives

The problem of incentives can really skew how much you can rely on someone else's circle of competence. This is particularly acute in the financial realm. Until recently, nearly all financial products we might be pushed into had commissions attached to them—in other words, our advisor made more money by giving us one set of advice than another, regardless of its wisdom. Fortunately, the rise of things like index funds of the stock and bond markets has mostly alleviated the issue.

In cases like financial advisory, we're not on solid ground until we know, in some detail, the compensation arrangement our advisor is under.

The same goes for buying furniture, buying a house, or buying a washing machine at a retail store. What does the knowledgeable advisor stand to gain from our purchase?

It goes beyond sales, of course. Whenever we are getting advice, it is from a person whose set of incentives is not the same as ours. It is not being cynical to know that this is the case, and to then act accordingly.

Suppose we want to take our car to a mechanic. Most of us, especially in this day and age, are complete Strangers in that land; we subsequently are open to be taken advantage of. There is not only an asymmetry in our general knowledge base about mechanics of a car, there is usually an asymmetry of knowledge about the actual current problem with the car. We haven't been under the hood, but the mechanic has. We know his incentive in this situation; it's to get us to spend as much as possible while still retaining us as a customer. The only solution, at least until we reach a certain level of trust with our mechanic, is to suck it up and learn a bit of the trade.

Fortunately, these days that is easy with the aid of the internet. And we don't need to learn it ahead of time. We can learn it on an as-needed basis. The way to do it, in this case, would be to defer all decisions on major spending until you've had time to poke around the resources you can find online and at least confirm that the mechanic isn't making a major bluff.

You can't see what's wrong but trust me.

experts in human psychology, implement technology without having the faintest idea how to fix it if something goes wrong, or design products with an imperfect understanding of our customers. These decisions may be outside our circles, but they still have to get made.

When Queen Elizabeth I of England* ascended to the throne, her reign was by no means assured. The tumultuous years under her father, brother, and sister had contributed to a political situation that was precarious at best. England was in a religious crisis that was threatening the stability of the kingdom, and was essentially broke.

Elizabeth knew there were aspects of leading the country that were outside her circle of competence. She had an excellent education and had spent most of her life just trying to survive. Perhaps that is why she was able to identify and admit to what she didn't know.

In her first speech as Queen, Elizabeth announced, "I mean to direct all my actions by good advice and counsel." [2] After outlining her intent upon becoming Queen, she proceeded to build her Privy Council—effectively the royal advisory board. She didn't copy her immediate predecessors, filling her council with yes men or wealthy incompetents who happen to have the same religious values. She blended the old and the new to develop stability and achieve continuity. She kept the group small so that real discussions could happen. She wanted a variety of opinions that could be challenged and debated. [3]

In large measure due to the advice she received from this council, advice that was the product of open debate that took in the circles of competence of each of the participants, Elizabeth took England from a country of civil unrest and frequent persecution to one that inspired loyalty and creativity in its citizens. She sowed the seeds for the empire that would eventually come to control one quarter of the globe.

*
Elizabeth I.
1533-1603 - Queen of England and Ireland. One of the most famous monarchs of all time, her image and legacy continue to capture the imagination. Elizabeth was a great orator, could speak about 11 languages, and wrote her own speeches and letters.

2
Tudor, Elizabeth.
"Wordes Spoken by the Queene to the Lordes." Speech to members of the House of Lords, Hatfield, November 20, 1558. National Archives. Retrieved from: http://www.nationalarchives.gov.uk/education/resources/elizabeth-monarchy/elizabeths-first-speech/

3
Brimacombe, Peter.
All the Queen's Men: The World of Elizabeth I. New York: St. Martin's Press, 2000.

—
Elizabeth I led her country at a time when very few women had
public positions of power. It is testament to her strength and
intelligence that she was able to admit what she didn't know and
take counsel from others.

1
Darwin, Charles.
The Descent of Man, and Selection in Relation to Sex. New York: D. Appleton and Company, 1882.

Conclusion

Critically, we must keep in mind that our circles of competence extend only so far. There are boundaries on the areas in which we develop the ability to make accurate decisions. In any given situation, there are people who have a circle, who have put in the time and effort to really understand the information.

It is also important to remember that no one can have a circle of competence that encompasses everything. There is only so much you can know with great depth of understanding. This is why being able to identify your circle, and knowing how to move around outside of it, is so important.

« Ignorance more often begets confidence than knowledge.»

Charles Darwin [1]

Staying in Your Circle

The idea a circle of competence in the realm of investments was stated very well by Berkshire Hathaway's Warren Buffett. When asked, he recommended that each individual stick to their area of special competence, and be very reluctant to stray. For when we stray too far, we get into areas where we don't even know what we don't know. We may not even know the questions we need to ask.

To explain his point, Buffett gives the example of a Russian immigrant woman who ran one of his businesses, the famous Nebraska Furniture Mart. The CEO, Rose Blumkin, spoke little English and could barely read or write, yet had a head for two things: numbers, and home furnishings. She stuck to those areas and built one of the country's great retailing establishments. Here it is in Buffett's words:

> I couldn't have given her $200 million worth of Berkshire Hathaway stock when I bought the business because she doesn't understand stock. She understands cash. She understands furniture. She understands real estate. She doesn't understand stocks, so she doesn't have anything to do with them. If you deal with Mrs. B in what I would call her circle of competence.... She is going to buy 5,000 end tables this afternoon (if the price is right). She is going to buy 20 different carpets in odd lots, and everything else like that [snaps fingers] because she understands carpets. She wouldn't buy 100 shares of General Motors if it was at 50 cents a share.[1]

Her iron focus on the things she knew best was largely responsible for her massive success in spite of the obstacles she faced.

1
Buffett, Warren.
Lecture to Notre Dame Faculty. South Bend, IN: 1991. Retrieved from:
https://www.tilsonfunds.com/BuffettNotreDame.pdf

Supporting Idea:
Falsifiability

Karl Popper wrote, "A theory is part of empirical science if and only if it conflicts with possible experiences[1] and is therefore in principle falsifiable by experience." The idea here is that if you can't prove something wrong, you can't really prove it right either.

Thus, in Popper's words, science requires testability: "If observation shows that the predicted effect is definitely absent, then the theory is simply refuted." This means a good theory must have an element of risk to it—namely, it has to risk being wrong. It must be able to be proven wrong under stated conditions.

In a true science, as opposed to a pseudo-science, the following statement can be easily made: "If x happens, it would show demonstrably that theory y is not true." We can then design an experiment, a physical one or sometimes a thought experiment, to figure out if x actually does happen. Falsification is the opposite of verification; you must try to show the theory is incorrect, and if you fail to do so, you actually strengthen it. To understand how this works in practice, think of evolution. As mutations appear, natural selection eliminates what doesn't work, thereby strengthening the fitness of the rest of the population.

Consider Popper's discussion of the concept of falsifiability in the context of Freud's psychoanalytic theory, which is broadly about the role of repressed childhood memories influencing our unconscious, in turn affecting our behavior. Popper was careful to say that it is not possible to prove that Freudianism was either true or not true, at least in part. We can say that we simply don't know whether it's true because it does not make specific testable predictions. It may have many kernels of truth in it, but we can't tell. The theory would have to be restated in a way to allow for experience to refute it.

Another interesting piece of Popper's work was an attack on what he called "historicism"—the idea that history has fixed laws or trends that inevitably lead to certain outcomes. This is where we use examples from the past to make definite conclusions about what is going to happen in the future.

Popper considered this kind of thinking pseudo-science, or worse—a dangerous ideology that tempts wannabe state planners and utopians to control society. He did not consider such historicist doctrines falsifiable. There is no way, for example, to test whether there is a Law of Increasing Technological Complexity in human society, which many are tempted to claim these days, because it is not actually a testable hypothesis. Instead of calling them interpretations, we call them

« A theory is part of empirical science if and only if it conflicts with possible experiences and is therefore in principle falsifiable by experience. »

Karl Popper

laws, or some similarly connotative word that implies an unchanging and universal state that is not open to debate, giving them an authority that they haven't earned. Too frequently, these postulated laws become immune to falsifying evidence—any new evidence is interpreted through the lens of the theory.

For example, we can certainly find confirmations for the idea that humans have progressed, in a specifically defined way, toward increasing technological complexity. But is that a Law of history, in the inviolable sense? Was it always going to be this way? No matter what the starting conditions or developments along the way, were humans always going to increase our technological prowess? We really can't say.

Here we hit on the problem of trying to assert any fundamental laws by which human history must inevitably progress. Trend is not destiny. Even if we can derive and understand certain laws of human biological nature, the trends of history itself are dependent on conditions, and conditions change.

Bertrand Russell's classic example of the chicken that gets fed every day is a great illustration of this concept.[2] Daily feedings have been going on for as long as the chicken has observed, and thus it supposes that these feedings are a guaranteed part of its life and will continue in perpetuity. The feedings appear as a law until the day the chicken gets its head chopped off. They are then revealed to be a trend, not a predictor of the future state of affairs.

Another way to look at it is how we tend to view the worst events in history. We tend to assume that the worst that has happened is the worst that can happen, and then prepare for that. We forget that "the worst" smashed a previous understanding of what was the worst. Therefore, we need to prepare more for the extremes allowable by physics rather than what has happened until now.

Applying the filter of falsifiability helps us sort through which theories are more robust. If they can't ever be proven false because we have no way of testing them, then the best we can do is try to determine their probability of being true.

1
Popper's theories on falsifiability are taken from his following works: *The Logic of Scientific Discovery, The Poverty of Historicism,* and *All Life is Problem Solving.*

2
Russell, Bertrand. *The Problems of Philosophy.* New York: Henry Holt and Company, 1912.

First Principles Thinking

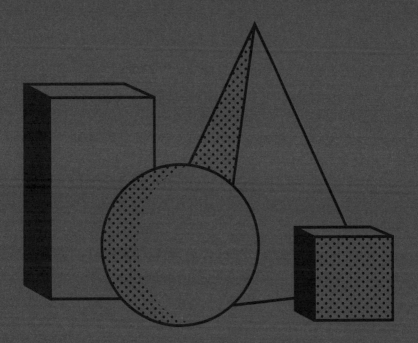

Go back to basics.

I don't know what's
the matter with people:
they don't learn
by understanding;
they learn by some
other way—by rote
or something. Their
knowledge is so fragile!

Richard Feynman[1]

First Principles Thinking

First principles thinking is one of the best ways to reverse-engineer complicated situations and unleash creative possibility. Sometimes called reasoning from first principles, it's a tool to help clarify complicated problems by separating the underlying ideas or facts from any assumptions based on them. What remain are the essentials. If you know the first principles of something, you can build the rest of your knowledge around them to produce something new.

The idea of building knowledge from first principles has a long tradition in philosophy. In the Western canon it goes back to Plato and Socrates[*], with significant contributions from Aristotle and Descartes. Essentially, they were looking for the foundational knowledge that would not change and that we could build everything else on, from our ethical systems to our social structures.

First principles thinking doesn't have to be quite so grand. When we do it, we aren't necessarily looking for absolute truths. Millennia of epistemological inquiry have shown us that these are hard to come by, and the scientific method has demonstrated that knowledge can only be built when we are actively trying to falsify it (see Supporting Idea: **Falsifiability**). Rather, first principles thinking identifies the elements that are, in the context of any given situation, non-reducible.

First principles do not provide a checklist of things that will always be true; our knowledge of first principles changes as we understand more. They are the foundation on which we must build, and thus will be different in every situation, but the more we know, the more we can challenge. For example, if we are considering how to improve the energy efficiency of a refrigerator, then the laws of thermodynamics can be taken as first principles. However, a theoretical chemist or physicist might want to explore entropy, and thus further break the

1
Leighton, Ralph.
Surely You're Joking, Mr. Feynman: Adventures of a Curious Character.
New York: Random House, 2014.

[*]
Socrates.
470-399 BCE - Greek philosopher. Famous for many philosophical conclusions, like "the only thing I know is that I know nothing", he didn't actually write any of his philosophy down; thus we have to thank those who came after, especially Plato, for preserving his legacy.

second law into its underlying principles and the assumptions that were made because of them. First principles are the boundaries that we have to work within in any given situation— so when it comes to thermodynamics an appliance maker might have different first principles than a physicist.

Techniques for establishing first principles

If we never learn to take something apart, test our assumptions about it, and reconstruct it, we end up bound by what other people tell us—trapped in the way things have always been done. When the environment changes, we just continue as if things were the same, making costly mistakes along the way.

Some of us are naturally skeptical of what we're told. Maybe it doesn't match up to our experiences. Maybe it's something that used to be true but isn't true anymore. And maybe we just think very differently about something. When it comes down to it, everything that is not a law of nature is just a shared belief. Money is a shared belief. So is a border. So are bitcoin. So is love. The list goes on.

If we want to identify the principles in a situation to cut through the dogma and the shared belief, there are two techniques we can use: Socratic questioning and the Five Whys.

Socratic questioning can be used to establish first principles through stringent analysis. This is a disciplined questioning process, used to establish truths, reveal underlying assumptions, and separate knowledge from ignorance. The key distinction between Socratic questioning and ordinary discussions is that the former seeks to draw out first principles in a systematic manner. Socratic questioning generally follows this process:

1. **Clarifying your thinking and explaining the origins of your ideas.** (Why do I think this? What exactly do I think?)
2. **Challenging assumptions.** (How do I know this is true? What if I thought the opposite?)

3.   **Looking for evidence.** (How can I back this up? What are the sources?)

4.   **Considering alternative perspectives**. (What might others think? How do I know I am correct?)

5.   **Examining consequences and implications.** (What if I am wrong? What are the consequences if I am?)

6.   **Questioning the original questions.** (Why did I think that? Was I correct? What conclusions can I draw from the reasoning process?)

Socratic questioning stops you from relying on your gut and limits strong emotional responses. This process helps you build something that lasts.

The Five Whys is a method rooted in the behavior of children. Children instinctively think in first principles. Just like us, they want to understand what's happening in the world. To do so, they intuitively break through the fog with a game some parents have come to dread, but which is exceptionally useful for identifying first principles: repeatedly asking "why?"

The goal of the Five Whys is to land on a "what" or "how". It is not about introspection, such as "Why do I feel like this?" Rather, it is about systematically delving further into a statement or concept so that you can separate reliable knowledge from assumption. If your "whys" result in a statement of falsifiable fact, you have hit a first principle. If they end up with a "because I said so" or "it just is", you know you have landed on an assumption that may be based on popular opinion, cultural myth, or dogma. These are not first principles.

There is no doubt that both of these methods slow us down in the short term. We have to pause, think, and research. They seem to get in the way of what we want to accomplish. And after we do them a couple of times we realize that after one or two questions, we are often lost. We actually don't know how to answer most of the questions. But when we are confronted with our own ignorance, we can't just give up or resort to self-defense. If we do, we will never identify the first principles we have to work with, and will instead make mistakes that will slow us down in the long term.

Warren, Robin.
1937 - Australian pathologist.
Marshall, Barry.
1951 - Australian physician.
They shared the Nobel Prize in
Physiology or Medicine in 2005.

1
Sagan, Carl.
"Why We Need To Understand
Science." *The Skeptical Inquirer*,
Vol.14, Issue 3 (Spring 1990).

2
Ashton, Kevin.
*How to Fly a Horse: The Secret
History of Creation, Invention,
and Discovery.* New York: Anchor
Books, 2015.

> «Science is much more than a body of knowledge. It is a way of thinking.»
>
> Carl Sagan [1]

First principles thinking as a way to blow past inaccurate assumptions

The discovery that a bacterium, not stress, actually caused the majority of stomach ulcers is a great example of what can be accomplished when we push past assumptions to get at first principles. Since the discovery of bacteria, scientists thought that bacteria could not grow in the stomach on account of the acidity. If you had surveyed both doctors and medical research scientists in the 60s or 70s, they likely would have postulated this as a first principle. When a patient came in complaining of stomach pain, no one ever looked for a bacterial cause.

It turned out, however, that a sterile stomach was not a first principle. It was an assumption. As Kevin Ashton writes in his book on creativity, discovery, and invention, "the dogma of the sterile stomach said that bacteria could not live in the gut."[2] Because this dogma was taken as truth, for a long time no one ever looked for reasons that it could be false.

That changed for good with the discovery of the *H. pylori* bacteria and its role in stomach ulcers. When pathologist Robin Warren* started seeing bacteria in samples from patients' stomachs, he realized that stomachs were not, in fact, sterile. He started collaborating with Barry Marshall*, a gastroenterologist, and together they started seeing bacteria in loads of stomachs. If the sterile stomach wasn't a first principle, then, when it came to stomachs, what was?

Grandin, Temple.
1947 - American professor of
animal science. In addition to
her contributions to livestock
welfare, she invented the "hug
box" device to calm those on
the autism spectrum. Autistic
herself, she is the subject of the
movie *Temple Grandin*, starring
Claire Danes.

3
Weintraub, Pamela.
"The Doctor Who Drank Infectious
Broth, Gave Himself an Ulcer,
and Solved a Medical Mystery."
Discover, March 2010.

Marshall, in an interview with *Discover*, recounts that Warren gave him a list of 20 patients identified as possibly having cancer, but when he had looked he had found the same bacteria in all of them instead. He said, "Why don't you look at their case records and see if they've got anything wrong with them." Since they now knew stomachs weren't sterile, they could question all the associated dogma about stomach disease and use some Socratic-type questioning to work to identify the first principles at play. They spent years challenging their related assumptions, clarifying their thinking, and looking for evidence.[3]

Their story ultimately has a happy ending—Marshall and Warren were awarded the Nobel Prize in 2005, and now stomach ulcers are regularly treated effectively with antibiotics, improving and saving the lives of millions of people. But many practitioners and scientists rejected their findings for decades. The dogma of the sterile stomach was so entrenched as a first principle, that it was hard to admit that it rested on some incorrect assumptions which ultimately ended with the explanation, "because that's just the way it is". Even though, as Ashton notes, "*H. pylori* has now been found in medical literature dating back to 1875," it was Warren and Marshall who were able to show that "because I said so" wasn't enough to count the sterile stomach as a first principle.

Incremental innovation and paradigm shifts

To improve something, we need to understand why it is successful or not. Otherwise, we are just copying thoughts or behaviors without understanding why they worked. First principles thinking helps us avoid the problem of relying on someone else's tactics without understanding the rationale behind them. Even incremental improvement is harder to achieve if we can't identify the first principles.

Temple Grandin* is famous for a couple of reasons. One, she is autistic, and was one of the first people to publicly disclose this fact and give insight into the inner workings of one type of autistic mind. Second, she is a scientist who has developed many techniques to improve the welfare of animals in the livestock industry.

One of the approaches she pioneered was the curved cattle chute. Previous to her experiments, cattle were put in a straight chute. Curved chutes, on the other hand, "are more efficient for handling cattle because they take advantage of the natural behavior of cattle. Cattle move through curved races more easily because they have a natural tendency to go back to where they came from."[1] Of course, science doesn't stop with one innovation, and animal scientists continue to study the best way to treat livestock animals.

Stockmanship Journal presented research that questioned the efficiency of Grandin's curved chute. It demonstrated that sometimes the much more simple straight chute would achieve the same effect in terms of cattle movement. The journal sought out Grandin's response, and it is invaluable for teaching us the necessity of first principles thinking.

Grandin explains that curved chutes are not a first principle. She designed them as a tactic to address the first principle of animal handling that she identified in her research—essentially that reducing stress to the animals is the single most important aspect and affects everything from conception rates to weight to immune systems. When designing a livestock environment, a straight chute could work as long as it is part of a system that reduces stress to the animals. You can change the tactics if you know the principles.[2]

Sometimes we don't want to fine-tune what is already there. We are skeptical, or curious, and are not interested in accepting what already exists as our starting point. So when we start with the idea that the way things are might not be the way they have to be, we put ourselves in the right frame of mind to identify first principles. The real power of first principles

1
http://www.grandin.com/design/design.html

2
Grandin, Temple. "A response to Hibbard and Locatelli." *Stockmanship Journal*, Vol. 3 No. 1 (January 2014).

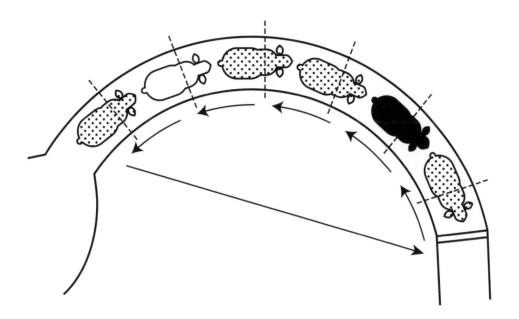

Curved cattle chutes improve animal welfare by working
with the natural behavior of the animals.

thinking is moving away from random change and into choices that have a real possibility of success.

Starting in the 1970s, scientists began to ask: what are the first principles of meat? The answers generally include taste, texture, smell, and use in cooking. Do you know what is not a first principle of meat? Once being a part of an animal. Perhaps most important to consumers is the taste. Less important is whether it was actually once part of a cow.

Researchers then looked at why meat tastes like meat. Part of the answer is a chemical reaction between sugars and amino acids during cooking, known as the Maillard reaction. This is what gives meat its flavor and smell. By replicating this exact reaction, scientists expect to be able to replicate the first principles of meat: taste and scent. In doing so they will largely eliminate the need to raise animals for consumption.

Instead of looking for ways to improve existing constructs, like mitigating the environmental impacts of the livestock industry, around 30 laboratories worldwide are now developing the means to grow artificial meat. This lab-grown meat is close to having the constituent parts of meat. One food researcher described the product this way:

> There is really a bite to it, there is quite some flavor with the browning. I know there is no fat in it so I didn't really know how juicy it would be, but there is … some intense taste; it's close to meat, it's not that juicy, but the consistency is perfect…. This is meat to me…it's really something to bite on and I think the look is quite similar.[1]

This quote illustrates how artificial meat combines the core properties of meat to form a viable replacement, thereby addressing some significant environmental and ethical concerns.

1
Ruetzler, Hanni, quoted in "What does a stem cell burger taste like?" by Melissa Hogenboom, BBCNews.com, August 5, 2013. Retrieved from: http://www.bbc.com/news/science-environment-23529841

2
Emerson, Harrington. Speech published in "The Convention: Fifteenth Annual Convention of the National Association of Clothiers, Held June 5 and 6, 1911." *The Clothier and Furnisher*, Volume 78, No 6 (July 1911).

«As to methods, there may be a million and then some, but principles are few. The man who grasps principles can successfully select his own methods. The man who tries methods, ignoring principles, is sure to have trouble.»

Harrington Emerson [2]

Conclusion

Reasoning from first principles allows us to step outside of history and conventional wisdom and see what is possible. When you really understand the principles at work, you can decide if the existing methods make sense. Often they don't.

Many people mistakenly believe that creativity is something that only some of us are born with, and either we have it or we don't. Fortunately, there seems to be ample evidence that this isn't true. We're all born rather creative, but during our formative years, it can be beaten out of us by busy parents and teachers. As adults, we rely on convention and what we're told because that's easier than breaking things down into first principles and thinking for yourself. Thinking through first principles is a way of taking off the blinders. Most things suddenly seem more possible.

Thought
Experiment

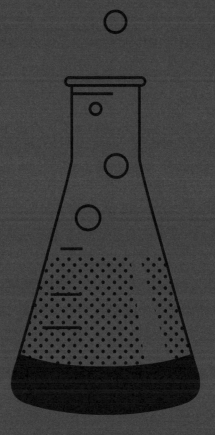

Imagine the possibilities.

Creativity is intelligence having fun.

Anonymous

Thought Experiment

Thought experiments can be defined as "devices of the imagination used to investigate the nature of things."[1] Many disciplines, such as philosophy and physics, make use of thought experiments to examine what can be known. In doing so, they can open up new avenues for inquiry and exploration. Thought experiments are powerful because they help us learn from our mistakes and avoid future ones. They let us take on the impossible, evaluate the potential consequences of our actions, and re-examine history to make better decisions. They can help us both figure out what we really want, and the best way to get there.

Betting on basketball

Suppose I asked you to tell me who would win in a game of basketball: The NBA champion LeBron James or the filmmaker Woody Allen? How much would you bet that your answer was correct?

I think you'd get me an answer pretty quickly, and I hope you'd bet all you had.

Next, suppose I asked you to tell me who'd win in a game of basketball: The NBA champion LeBron James or the NBA champion Kevin Durant? How much would you bet that your answer was correct?

A little harder, right? Would you bet anywhere near all you had on being right?

Let's think this through. You attempted to solve both of the questions in the same way—you imagined the contests. Perhaps more importantly, you *didn't* attempt to solve either of them by calling up Messrs. James, Allen, and Durant and inviting them over for an afternoon of basketball. You simply simulated them in your mind.

In the first case, your knowledge of James (young, tall,

1
Brown, James Robert and Fehige, Yiftach, "Thought Experiments", *The Stanford Encyclopedia of Philosophy* (Summer 2017 Edition), Edward N. Zalta (ed.). Retrieved from: https://plato.stanford.edu/entries/thought-experiment/

athletic, and skilled), Allen (old, small, frail, and funny), and the game of basketball gave you a clear mental image. The disparity between the players' abilities makes the question (and the bet) a total no-brainer.

In the second case, your knowledge of LeBron and Durant may well be extensive, but that doesn't make it an easy bet. They're both professional basketball players who are quite similar in size and ability, and both of them are likely to go down as among the best ever to play the game. It's doubtful that one is *much* better than the other in a one-on-one match. The only way to answer for sure would be to see them play. And even then, a one-off contest is not going to be definitive.

A better way to answer the "who would win" question is through a remarkable ability of the human brain—the ability to conduct a detailed thought experiment. Its chief value is that it lets us do things in our heads we cannot do in real life, and so explore situations from more angles than we can physically examine and test for.

Thought experiments are more than daydreaming. They require the same rigor as a traditional experiment in order to be useful. Much like the scientific method, a thought experiment generally has the following steps:

1. Ask a question
2. Conduct background research
3. Construct hypothesis
4. Test with (thought) experiments
5. Analyze outcomes and draw conclusions
6. Compare to hypothesis and adjust accordingly (new question, etc.)

In the James/Allen experiment above, we started with a question: Who would win in a game of basketball? If you didn't already know who those people were, finding out would have

Who would win in a game of one-on-one?

been a necessary piece of background research. Then you came out with your hypothesis (James all the way!), and you thought it through.

One of the real powers of the thought experiment is that there is no limit to the number of times you can change a variable to see if it influences the outcome. In order to place that bet, you would want to estimate in how many possible basketball games does Woody Allen beat LeBron James. Out of 100,000 game scenarios, Allen probably only wins in the few where LeBron starts the game by having a deadly heart attack. Experimenting to discover the full spectrum of possible outcomes gives you a better appreciation for what you can influence and what you can reasonably expect to happen.

Let's now explore few areas in which thought experiments are tremendously useful.

1.   Imagining physical impossibilities
2.   Re-imagining history
3.   Intuiting the non-intuitive

Imagining physical impossibilities: Albert Einstein was a great user of the thought experiment because it is a way to logically carry out a test in one's own head that would be very difficult or impossible to perform in real life. With this tool, we can solve problems with intuition and logic that cannot be demonstrated physically.

One of his notable thought experiments involved an elevator.[1] Imagine you were in a closed elevator, feet glued to the floor. Absent any other information, would you be able to know whether the elevator was in outer space with a string pulling the elevator upwards at an accelerating rate, or sitting on Earth, being pulled down by gravity? By running the thought experiment, Einstein concluded that you would not.

This led to the formulation of Einstein's second major theory, the general theory of relativity—his universal theory of

1
Isaacson, Walter.
Einstein: His Life and Universe.
New York: Simon and Schuster,
2007.

gravity. Einstein's hypothesis was that the force you felt from acceleration and the force you felt from gravity didn't just *feel* the same—they were the same! Gravity must work similarly to the accelerating elevator. We can't build elevators in space, but can still define some of the properties they would have if we could. This gives us enough information to test the hypothesis. Eventually, Einstein worked it all out mathematically and in great detail, but it started with a simple thought experiment, impossible to actually perform.

This type of thought experiment need not only apply to physics and is actually reflected in some of our common expressions. When we say "if money were no object" or "if you had all the time in the world," we are asking someone to conduct a thought experiment because actually removing that variable (money or time) is physically impossible. In reality, money is always an object, and we never have all the time in the world. But the act of detailing out the choices we would make in these alternate realities that have otherwise similar properties to our current one, doing the thought experiment, is what leads to insights regarding what we value in life and where to focus our energies. — Sidebar: The Trolley Experiment

Re-imagining history: A familiar use of the thought experiment is to re-imagine history. This one we all use, all the time. What if I hadn't been stuck at the airport bar where I met my future business partner? Would World War I have started if Gavrilo Princip hadn't shot the Archduke of Austria in Sarajevo? If Cleopatra hadn't found a way to meet Caesar, would she still have been able to take the throne of Egypt?

These approaches are called the *historical counter-factual and semi-factual.* If Y happened instead of X, what would the outcome have been? Would the outcome have been the same?

As popular—and generally useful—as counter- and semi-factuals are, they are also the areas of thought

The Trolley Experiment

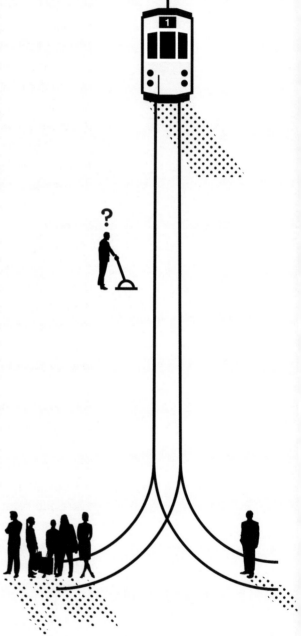

Thought experiments are often used to explore ethical and moral issues. When you are dealing with questions of life and death it is obviously not recommended to kill a bunch of people in order to determine the most ethical course of action. This then is where a thought experiment is also extremely valuable.

One of the most famous of this type is the trolley experiment. It goes like this: say you are the driver of a trolley that is out of control. You apply the brakes and nothing happens. Ahead of you are five people who will die should your trolley continue on the track. At the last moment you notice a spur that has one person on it. What do you do? Do you continue on and kill the five, or do you divert and kill the one?

This experiment was first proposed in modern form by Philippa Foot in her paper "The Problem of Abortion and the Doctrine of the Double Effect,"[1] and further considered extensively by Judith Jarvis Thomson in "The Trolley Problem."[2] In both cases the value of the thought experiment is clear. The authors were able to explore situations that would be physically impossible to reproduce without causing serious harm, and in so doing significantly advanced certain questions of morality. Moreover, the trolley problem remains relevant to this day as technological advances often ask us to define when it is acceptable, and even desirable, to sacrifice one to save many (and lest you think this is always the case, Thomson conducts another great thought experiment considering a doctor killing one patient to save five through organ donation).

1
Foot, Philippa.
"The Problem of Abortion and the Doctrine of the Double Effect." *Oxford Review*, No. 5 (1967).

2
Thomson, Judith Jarvis.
"The Trolley Problem." *Yale Law Journal*, Vol. 94, No. 6 (May, 1985).

experiment with which we need to use the most caution. Why? Because history is what we call a chaotic system. A small change in the beginning conditions can cause a *very* different outcome down the line. This is where the rigor of the scientific method is indispensable if we want to draw conclusions that are actually useful.

To understand it, let's think about another chaotic system we're all familiar with, the weather. Why is it that we can predict the movement of the stars but we can't predict the weather more than a few weeks out, and even that is not altogether reliable?

It's because weather is highly chaotic. Any infinitesimally small error in our calculations today will change the result down the line, as rapid feedback loops occur throughout time. Since our measurement tools are not infinitely accurate, and never will be, we are stuck with the unpredictability of chaotic systems.

And compared to human systems, one could say weather is pretty reliable stuff. As anyone who's seen *Back to the Future* knows, a small change in the past could have a massive, unpredictable effect on the future. Thus, running historical counter-factuals is an easy way to accidentally mislead yourself. We simply don't know what else would have occurred had Cleopatra not met Caesar or had you not been stuck at that airport. The potential outcomes are too chaotic.

But we can use thought experiments to *explore* unrealized outcomes—to re-run a process as many times as we like to see what could have occurred, and learn more about the limits we have to work with.

The truth is, the events that have happened in history are but one realization of the historical process—one possible outcome among a large variety of possible outcomes. They're like a deck of cards that has been dealt out only one time. All the things that didn't happen, but could have if some little thing went another way, are invisible to us. That is, until we use our brains to generate these theoretical worlds via thought experiments.

If we can also factor in the approximate probability of these occurrences, relative to the scope of possible ones, we can learn what the most likely outcomes are. Sometimes it is easy to imagine ten different ways a situation could have played out differently, but more of a stretch to change the variables and still end up with the same thing.

So let's try it. First, we have to ask a question. What if Serbian Gavrilo Princip hadn't shot Austrian Archduke Franz Ferdinand? That single act has often been credited with launching World War I, so it is a question worth asking. If we conclude the assassination started a chain reaction for which war was the inevitable result, it would certainly tell us a lot about certain causal relationships in politics, diplomacy, and possibly human psychology.

Then we need to do our background research: What do we need to know to be able to answer this question? So we look into it—treaties, conflicts, alliances, interests, personalities—enough to be able to formulate an hypothesis.

An immediate response to the assassination was on June 30, 1914, two days later. Austria changed its policy toward Serbia. Shortly after that Germany offered full military support to Austria, and less than two months later the world was at war. Thus, a next step in our thought experiment might be to refine the question. Something like, how did Princip's assassination of the Archduke influence Austrian policy toward Serbia?

Our hypothesis could be one of the following:
1.   The assassination had no effect on the policy
2.   The assassination had partial effect on the policy
3.   The assassination had total effect on the policy

To test any one of these, we run the experiment in our heads. We sit back and think about what the world looked like in

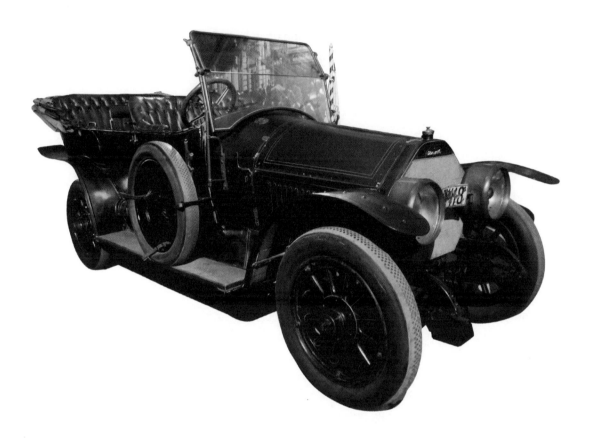

What we think of as an inevitable occurrence could have played out in many ways: Earlier on the day of the assassination, Archduke Ferdinand and his wife Sophie survived a grenade being detonated by their car. It was on the way to visit those injured, an unplanned change of schedule, that Princip got his opportunity.

Sarajevo on June 28, 1914. The Archduke and his wife being chauffeured in their car, Gavrilo Princip cleaning his gun somewhere. Now we imagine Princip gets stomach cramps from some bad food the night before. The Archduke's car makes it to its destination while Princip is curled up in bed. The Archduke gives a speech, emphasizing peace. One of Princip's gang tries to assassinate the Archduke, but fails. How does Austria react? Is it demonstrably different from what they actually did?

Princip wasn't a lone wolf, and there was a lot of unrest in Serbia towards Austria. How could the situation be changed to lead to different Austrian policy? Given the climate at the time, is our hypothetical situation realistic? Meaning, can you construct an historically accurate scenario in which no events come to pass that prompt Austria's policy change? How many Serbians would have to get the stomach flu?

One of the goals of a thought experiment like this is to understand the situation enough to identify the decisions and actions that had impact. This process doesn't provide definitive answers, such as whether the assassination did, or did not, cause World War I. What you are trying to get to is a rough idea of how much it may have contributed to starting the war. The more scenarios you can imagine where war comes to pass without the assassination, the weaker the case for it being the critical cause. Thus, by exploring the realistic relationships between events you can better understand the most likely effects of any one decision. — Sidebar: Reduce the Role of Chance

Intuiting the non-intuitive: One of the uses of thought experiments is to improve our ability to intuit the non-intuitive. In other words, a thought experiment allows us to verify if our natural intuition is correct by running experiments in our deliberate, conscious minds that make a point clear.

Reduce the Role of Chance

Let's try a real world example. Suppose you were to buy $100,000 of stock in Google, with 50% paid for in cash and 50% borrowed from the brokerage firm. (They call it a margin loan.)

A few years later, the stock price has doubled: That means your $100,000 is worth $200,000. Since you still owe the brokerage $50,000, your own $50,000 is now worth $150,000—you've tripled your money! You consider yourself a financial genius.

Before we land on that conclusion, though, let's run our Theoretical World Generator a bunch of times in our head. What else could have happened, but didn't?

Google could have gone down 50% before it went up 100%—nearly all stocks on the exchange have had this happen to them at some time or another. In fact, Google could have gone down 90%! The whole New York Stock Exchange did just that between 1929 and 1932.

What if something like that had happened? The brokerage would have called in your margin loan: Game over, thanks for playing. You would have been worth zero.

Now, return to the beginning of the chapter again. If you're going to buy Google on margin, is your bet that Google won't go down 50% more similar to the LeBron/Allen thought experiment, or the LeBron/Durant thought experiment? Running through the scenario 100,000 times, how many times do you go broke and how many times do you triple your dough?

This gives you some real decision-making power: It tells you about the limits of what you know and the limits of what you should attempt. It tells you, in an imprecise but useful way, a lot about how smart or stupid your decisions were regardless of the actual outcome. It makes you aware of your process, so that even if the results are good, you can recognize when this was all down to luck and that maybe you should work on your decision-making process to reduce the role of chance.

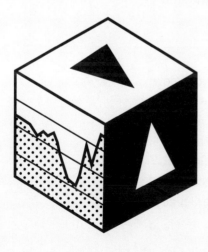

An example of this is the famous "veil of ignorance" proposed by philosopher John Rawls in his influential *Theory of Justice*. In order to figure out the most fair and equitable way to structure society, he proposed that the designers of said society operate behind a veil of ignorance. This means that they could not know who they would be in the society they were creating. If they designed the society without knowing their economic status, their ethnic background, talents and interests, or even their gender, they would have to put in place a structure that was as fair as possible in order to guarantee the best possible outcome for themselves.[1]

Our initial intuition of what is fair is likely to be challenged during the "veil of ignorance" thought experiment. When confronted with the question of how best to organize society, we have this general feeling that it should be fair. But what exactly does this mean? We can use this thought experiment to test the likely outcomes of different rules and structures to come up with an aggregate of "most fair."

We need not be constructing the legislation of entire nations for this type of thinking to be useful. Think, for example, of a company's human resources policies on hiring, office etiquette, or parental leave. What kind of policies would you design or support if you didn't know what your role in the company was? Or even anything about who you were?

Conclusion

Thought experiments tell you about the limits of what you know and the limits of what you should attempt. In order to improve our decision-making and increase our chances of success, we must be willing to probe all of the possibilities we can think of. Thought experiments are not daydreams. They require both rigor and work. But the more you use them, the more you understand actual cause and effect, and the more knowledge you have of what can really be accomplished.

*
Rawls, John.
1921-2002 - American moral and political philosopher. His work theorized "Justice and fairness" and remains integral to discussions of political philosophy.

1
Rawls, John.
A Theory of Justice, revised edition. Cambridge: Harvard University Press, 2005.

Supporting Idea:

Necessity and Sufficiency

We often make the mistake of assuming that having some necessary conditions in place means that we have all of the sufficient conditions in place for our desired event or effect to occur. The gap between the two is the difference between becoming a published author and becoming J.K. Rowling. Certainly you have to know how to write well to become either, but it isn't sufficient to become a Rowling. This is somewhat obvious to most. What's not obvious is that the gap between what is necessary to succeed and what is sufficient is often luck, chance, or some other factor beyond your direct control.

Assume you wanted to make it into the Fortune 500. Capital is necessary, but not sufficient. Hard work is necessary, but not sufficient. Intelligence is necessary, but not sufficient. Billionaire success takes all of those things and more, plus a lot of luck. That's a big reason that there's no recipe.

Winning a military battle is a great example of necessity and sufficiency. It is necessary to prepare for the battle by evaluating the strength and tactics of your enemy, and by developing your own plan. You need to address logistics such as supplies, and have a comprehensive strategy that allows flexibility to respond to the unexpected. These things, however, are not enough to win the battle. Without them you definitely won't be successful, but on their own they are not sufficient for success.

This concept is demonstrated in sport as well. To be successful at a professional level in any sport depends on some necessary conditions. You must be physically capable of meeting the demands of that sport, and have the time and means to train. Meeting these conditions, however, is not sufficient to guarantee a successful outcome. Many hard-working, talented athletes are unable to break into the professional ranks.

In mathematics they call these sets. The set of conditions necessary to become successful is a part of the set that is sufficient to become successful. But the sufficient set itself is far larger than the necessary set. Without that distinction, it's too easy for us to be misled by the wrong stories.

Second-Order Thinking

—
What happens next?

Technology is fine,
but the scientists and
engineers only partially
think through their
problems. They solve
certain aspects, but
not the total, and as
a consequence it is
slapping us back in the
face very hard.

Barbara McClintock[1]

Second-Order Thinking

Almost everyone can anticipate the immediate results of their actions. This type of first-order thinking is easy and safe but it's also a way to ensure you get the same results that everyone else gets. Second-order thinking is thinking farther ahead and thinking holistically. It requires us to not only consider our actions and their immediate consequences, but the subsequent effects of those actions as well. Failing to consider the second- and third-order effects can unleash disaster.

It is often easier to find examples of when second-order thinking didn't happen—when people did not consider the effects of the effects. When they tried to do something good, or even just benign, and instead brought calamity, we can safely assume the negative outcomes weren't factored into the original thinking. Very often, the second level of effects is not considered until it's too late. This concept is often referred to as the "Law of Unintended Consequences" for this very reason.

We see examples of this throughout history. During their colonial rule of India, the British government began to worry about the number of venomous cobras in Delhi. To reduce the numbers, they instituted a reward for every dead snake brought to officials. In response, Indian citizens dutifully complied and began breeding the snakes to slaughter and bring to officials. The snake problem was worse than when it started because the British officials didn't think at the second level. Second-order effects occur even with something simple like adding traction on tires: it seems like such a great idea because the more you have the less likely you are to slide, the faster you can stop, and thus the safer you are. However, the second-order effects are that your engine has to work harder to propel the car, you get worse gas mileage (releasing more detrimental carbon dioxide into the atmosphere), and you leave more rubber particles on the road.

1
Keller, Evelyn Fox.
A Feeling for the Organism: The Life and Work of Barbara McClintock.
New York: W.H. Freeman and Company, 1983.

First-Order
Consequences

2nd
Order

3rd
Order

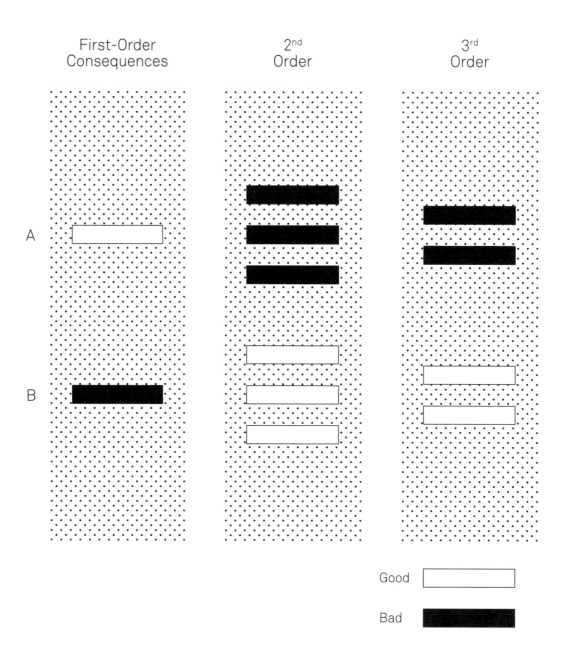

Good

Bad

1
Atwood, Margaret.
Surfacing. Toronto: McClelland
and Stewart, 1972.

*
Hardin, Garrett.
1915-2003 - American ecologist
and philosopher. The common
thread in his work was an interest
in bioethics.

2
Hardin, Garrett.
Living Within Limits. New York:
Oxford University Press, 1993.

This is why any comprehensive thought process considers the effects of the effects as seriously as possible. You are going to have to deal with them anyway. The genie never gets back in the bottle. You can never delete consequences to arrive at the original starting conditions.

«Stupidity is the same as evil if you judge by the results.»

Margaret Atwood [1]

In an example of second-order thinking deficiency, we have been feeding antibiotics to livestock for decades to make the meat safer and cheaper. Only in recent years have we begun to realize that in doing so we have helped create bacteria that we cannot defend against.

In 1963, the UC Santa Barbara ecologist and economist Garrett Hardin[*] proposed his First Law of Ecology: "You can never merely do one thing." [2] We operate in a world of multiple, overlapping connections, like a web, with many significant, yet obscure and unpredictable, relationships. He developed second-order thinking into a tool, showing that if you don't consider "the effects of the effects," you can't really claim to be doing any thinking at all.

When it comes to the overuse of antibiotics in meat, the first-order consequence is that the animals gain more weight per pound of food consumed, and thus there is profit for the farmer. Animals are sold by weight, so the less food you have to use to bulk them up, the more money you will make when you go to sell them.

The second-order effects, however, have many serious, negative consequences. The bacteria that survive this continued antibiotic exposure are antibiotic resistant. That means that the agricultural industry, when using these antibiotics as bulking agents, is allowing mass numbers of drug-resistant bacteria to become part of our food chain.

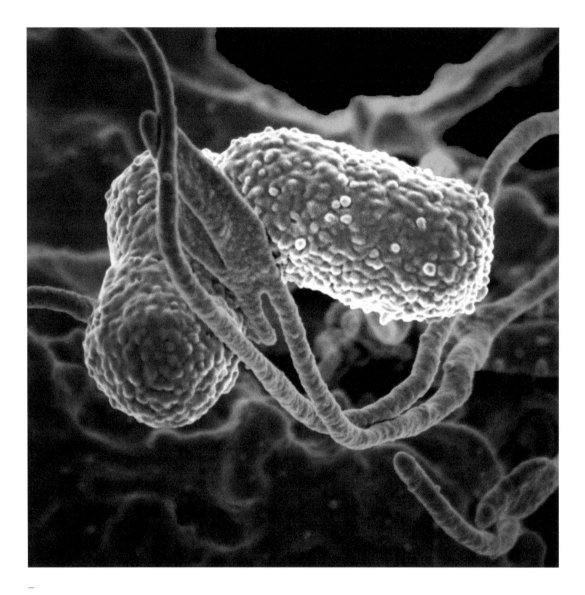

—
Effect of effects: the original purpose of using antibiotics
to increase cattle size led to the unintended negative
consequence of creating an environment which lets drug-
resistant bacteria thrive.

1

Muir, John.
My First Summer in the Sierra.
Boston: Houghton Mifflin, 1911.

High degrees of connections make second-order think-ing all the more critical, because denser webs of relationships make it easier for actions to have far-reaching consequences. You may be focused in one direction, not recognizing that the consequences are rippling out all around you. Things are not produced and consumed in a vacuum.

«When we try to pick out anything by itself, we find it hitched to everything else in the Universe.»

John Muir [1]

Second-order thinking is not a way to predict the future. You are only able to think of the likely consequences based on the information available to you. However, this is not an excuse to power ahead and wait for post-facto scientific analysis.

Could these consequences of putting antibiotics in the feed of all animals have been anticipated? Likely, yes, by any-one with even a limited understanding of biology. We know that organisms evolve. They adapt based on environmental pres-sures, and those with shorter life cycles can do it quite quickly because they have more opportunities. Antibiotics, by defini-tion, kill bacteria. Bacteria, just like all other living things, want to survive. The pressures put on them by continued exposure to antibiotics increase their pace of evolution. Over the course of many generations, eventually mutations will occur that allow certain bacteria to resist the effects of the antibiotics. These are the ones that will reproduce more rapidly, creating the situ-ation we are now in. — Sidebar: Second-Order Problem

Second-order thinking teaches us two important concepts that underlie the use of this model. If we're interested in under-standing how the world really works, we must include second and subsequent effects. We must be as observant and honest

Second-Order Problem

Warren Buffett used a very apt metaphor once to describe how the second-order problem is best described by a crowd at a parade: Once a few people decide to stand on their tip-toes, everyone has to stand on their tip-toes. No one can see any better, but they're all worse off.

—
Buffett, Warren.
"Letter to Shareholders, 1985."
BerkshireHathaway.com. Retrieved
from: http://www.berkshirehatha-
way.com/letters/1985.html

Cleopatra VII Philopator.
69-30 BCE - She was the last
Ptolemy to rule Egypt and has
been talked about ever since. The
subject of numerous biographies,
histories, plays, and movies, she
is one of history's true legends.

1
Schiff, Stacy.
Cleopatra: A Life. New York: Back
Bay Books, 2010.

as we can about the web of connections we are operating in. How often is short-term gain worth protracted long-term pain?

Let's look at two areas where second-order thinking can be used to great benefit:

1. **Prioritizing long-term interests over immediate gains**
2. **Constructing effective arguments**

Second-order thinking and realizing long-term interests:
This is a useful model for seeing past immediate gains to identify long-term effects we want. This is often a conflict for us, as when we choose to forgo the immediate pleasure of candy to improve our long-term health. The first-order effect is this amazing feeling triggered by pure sugar. But what are the second-order effects of regular candy consumption? Is this what I want my body or life to look like in ten years? Second-order thinking involves asking ourselves if what we are doing now is going to get us the results we want.

Finding historical examples of second-order thinking can be tricky because we don't want to evaluate based solely on the outcome: "It all turned out well, so he must have thought through the consequences of his actions." Even if you can glimpse the long-term gain from your short-term pain, there is no guarantee you are going to get there.

In 48 BC, Cleopatra* of Egypt was in a terrible position.[1] Technically co-regent with her brother, in a family famous for murdering siblings, she was encamped in a swampy desert, ousted from the palace, stuck with no solid plan for how to get back. She was Queen, but had made a series of unpopular decisions which left her with little support, and which gave her brother ample justification for trying to have her assassinated. What to do?

At the same time the great Roman general Caesar arrived in Egypt, chasing down his enemy Pompey and making sure the Egyptians knew who really was in charge on the

In order to meet Caesar and develop an alliance, yet barred from
the palace, Cleopatra organized an elaborate plot to smuggle
herself in wrapped in a cloth and stuffed in a basket.

Mediterranean. Egypt was an incredibly fertile, wealthy country, and as such was of great importance to the Romans. The way they inserted themselves in Egypt, however, made them extremely unpopular there.

In order to survive, Cleopatra had to make some decisions. Should she try to work things out with her brother? Should she try to marshal some support from another country? Or should she try to align herself with Caesar?

In *Cleopatra: A Life*, Stacy Schiff explains that even in 48 BC at the age of 21, Cleopatra would have had a superb political education, based on both historical knowledge and firsthand exposure to the tumultuous events of life on the Mediterranean. She would have observed actions taken by her father, Auletes, as well as various family members, that resulted in exile, bribery, and murder from either the family, the Romans, or the populace. She would have known that there were no easy answers. As Schiff explains, "What Auletes passed down to his daughter was a precarious balancing act. To please one constituency was to displease another. Failure to comply with Rome would lead to intervention. Failure to stand up to Rome would lead to riots."

In this situation it was thus imperative that Cleopatra consider the second-order effects of her actions. Short-term gain might easily lead to execution (as indeed it already had for many of her relatives). If she wanted to be around for a while, she needed to balance her immediate goals of survival and the throne, with the future need for support to stay on it.

In 48 BC Cleopatra chose to align herself with Caesar. It seems likely she would have known the first-order effects of this decision: Namely that it would anger her brother, who would increase his plotting to have her killed, and that it would anger the Egyptian people, who didn't want a Roman involved in their affairs. She probably anticipated that there would be short-term pain, and there was. Cleopatra effectively started a civil war, with a siege on the palace that left her and Caesar

Developing Trust for Future Success

T rust and trustworthiness are the results of multiple interactions. This is why second-order thinking is so useful and valuable. Going for the immediate payoff in our interactions with people, unless they are a win-win, almost always guarantees that interaction will be a one-off. Maximizing benefits is something that happens over time. Thus, considering the effects of the effects of our actions on others, or on our reputations, is critical to getting people to trust us, and to enjoy the benefits of cooperation that come with that.

–

To learn more about how we build trust in relationships see:
Ostrom, Elinor and Walker, James, eds. *Trust and Reciprocity: Interdisciplinary Lessons from Experimental Research*. New York: Russell Sage Foundation, 2003.

trapped there for months. In addition, she had to be constantly vigilant against the assassination schemes of her brother. So why did she do it?

In reality we will never know for sure. We can only make an educated guess. But given that Cleopatra ruled Egypt quite successfully for many years after these events, her decision was based on seeing the effects of the effects. If she could somehow make it through the short-term pain, then her leadership had much greater chances of being successful with the support of Caesar and Rome than without it. As Schiff notes, "The Alexandrian War gave Cleopatra everything she wanted. It cost her little." In winning the civil war Caesar got rid of all major opposition to Cleopatra and firmly aligned himself with her reign.

Being aware of second-order consequences and using them to guide your decision-making may mean the short term is less spectacular, but the payoffs for the long term can be enormous. By delaying gratification now, you will save time in the future. You won't have to clean up the mess you made on account of not thinking through the effects of your short-term desires. — Sidebar: Developing Trust for Future Success

Constructing an effective argument: Second-order thinking can help you avert problems and anticipate challenges that you can then address in advance.

For example, most of us have to construct arguments every day. Convincing your boss to take a chance on a new form of outreach, convincing your spouse to try a new parenting technique. Life is filled with the need to be persuasive. Arguments are more effective when we demonstrate that we have considered the second-order effects and put effort into verifying that these are desirable as well.

In late 18th-century England, women had very few rights. Philosopher Mary Wollstonecraft* was frustrated that this lack of rights limited a woman's ability to be independent and make choices on how to live her life. Instead of arguing, however, for why women should get rights, she recognized that she had to demonstrate the value that these rights would confer. She explained the benefits to society that would be realized as a result of those rights. She argued for the education of women because this would in turn make them better wives and mothers, more able to both support themselves and raise smart, conscientious children.

Her thoughts, from *A Vindication of the Rights of Woman*, are a demonstration of second-order thinking:

> *Asserting the rights which women in common with men ought to contend for, I have not attempted to extenuate their faults; but to prove them to be the natural consequence of their education and station in society. If so, it is reasonable to suppose that they will change their character, and correct their vices and follies, when they are allowed to be free in a physical, moral, and civil sense.*[1]

Empowering women was a first-order effect of recognizing that women had rights. But by discussing the logical consequences this would have on society, the second-order effects, she started a conversation that eventually resulted in what we now call feminism. Not only would women get freedoms they deserved, they would become better women, and better members of society.

A word of caution

Second-order thinking, as valuable as it is, must be tempered in one important way: You can't let it lead to the paralysis of the Slippery Slope Effect, the idea that if we start with action A, everything after is a slippery slope down to hell, with a chain of consequences B, C, D, E, and F.

Garrett Hardin smartly addresses this in *Filters Against Folly*:

> *Those who take the wedge (Slippery Slope) argument with the utmost seriousness act as though they think human*

Wollstonecraft, Mary. 1759-1797 - English writer and philosopher. She wrote a huge variety of works, from novels and histories to philosophy and children's books. Her daughter Mary Shelley wrote Frankenstein.

1

Wollstonecraft, Mary. *A Vindication of the Rights of Woman*. London: 1792.

1
Hardin, Garrett.
Filters Against Folly. New York:
Penguin, 1985.

beings are completely devoid of practical judgment. Countless examples from everyday life show the pessimists are wrong…If we took the wedge argument seriously, we would pass a law forbidding all vehicles to travel at any speed greater than zero. That would be an easy way out of the moral problem. But we pass no such law.[1]

In practical life, everything has limits. Even if we consider second and subsequent effects, we can only go so far. During waves of Prohibition fever in the United States and elsewhere, conservative abstainers have frequently made the case that even taking the *first* drink would be the first step towards a life of sin. They're right: It's true that drinking a beer *might* lead you to become an alcoholic. But not most of the time.

Thus we need to avoid the slippery slope and the analysis paralysis it can lead to. Second-order thinking needs to evaluate the most likely effects and their most likely consequences, checking our understanding of what the typical results of our actions will be. If we worried about all possible effects of effects of our actions, we would likely never do anything, and we'd be wrong. How you'll balance the need for higher-order thinking with practical, limiting judgment must be taken on a case-by-case basis.

Conclusion

We don't make decisions in a vacuum and we can't get something for nothing. When making choices, considering consequences can help us avoid future problems. We must ask ourselves the critical question: And then what?

Consequences come in many varieties, some more tangible than others. Thinking in terms of the system in which you are operating will allow you to see that your consequences have consequences. Thinking through a problem as far as you can with the information you have allows us to consider time, scale, thresholds, and more. And weighing different paths is what thinking is all about. A little time spent thinking ahead can save us massive amounts of time later.

Probabilistic Thinking

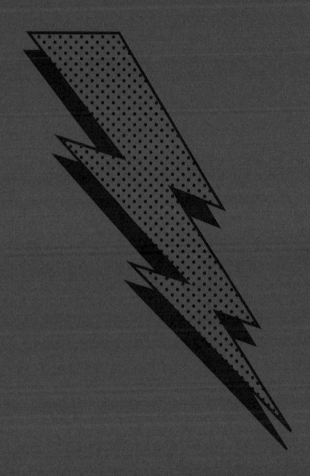

—
What are the chances?

The theory of probability is the only mathematical tool available to help map the unknown and the uncontrollable. It is fortunate that this tool, while tricky, is extraordinarily powerful and convenient.

Benoit Mandelbrot[1]

Probabilistic Thinking

Probabilistic thinking is essentially trying to estimate, using some tools of math and logic, the likelihood of any specific outcome coming to pass. It is one of the best tools we have to improve the accuracy of our decisions. In a world where each moment is determined by an infinitely complex set of factors, probabilistic thinking helps us identify the most likely outcomes. When we know these our decisions can be more precise and effective.

Are you going to get hit by lightning or not?

Why we need the concept of probabilities at all is worth thinking about. Things either are or are not, right? We either *will* get hit by lightning today or we *won't.* The problem is, we just don't know until we live out the day. Which doesn't help us at all when we make our decisions in the morning. The future is far from determined and we can better navigate it by understanding the likelihood of events that could impact us.

Our lack of perfect information about the world gives rise to all of probability theory, and its usefulness. We know now that the future is inherently unpredictable because not all variables can be known and even the smallest error imaginable in our data very quickly throws off our predictions. The best we can do is estimate the future by generating realistic, useful probabilities. So how do we do that?

Probability is everywhere, down to the very bones of the world. The probabilistic machinery in our minds—the cut-to-the-quick *heuristics* made so famous by the psychologists Daniel Kahneman and Amos Tversky—was evolved by the human species in a time before computers, factories, traffic, middle managers, and the stock market. It served us in a time when human life was about *survival*, and still serves us well in that capacity.[2]

1

Mandelbrot, Benoit.
The Fractal Geometry of Nature.
New York: W.H. Freeman and Company, 1977.

2

Kahneman, Daniel and Tversky, Amos. *Judgment under Uncertainty: Heuristics and Biases.* Science. Volume 185, 1974.

But what about today—a time when, for most of us, survival is not so much the issue? We want to *thrive*. We want to compete, and win. Mostly, we want to make good decisions in complex social systems that were not part of the world in which our brains evolved their (quite rational) heuristics.

For this, we need to consciously add in a needed layer of probability awareness. What is it and how can I use it to my advantage?

There are three important aspects of probability that we need to explain so you can integrate them into your thinking to get into the ballpark and improve your chances of catching the ball:

1.   **Bayesian thinking**
2.   **Fat-tailed curves**
3.   **Asymmetries**

Thomas Bayes and Bayesian thinking: Bayes[*] was an English minister in the first half of the 18th century, whose most famous work, "An Essay Toward Solving a Problem in the Doctrine of Chances", was brought to the attention of the Royal Society by his friend Richard Price in 1763—two years after his death. The essay concerned how we should adjust probabilities when we encounter new data, and provided the seeds for the great mathematician Pierre Simon Laplace to develop what we now call Bayes's Theorem.

The core of Bayesian thinking (or Bayesian updating, as it can be called) is this: given that we have limited but useful information about the world, and are constantly encountering new information, we should probably take into account what we already know when we learn something new. As much of it as possible. Bayesian thinking allows us to use all relevant prior information in making decisions. Statisticians might call it a *base rate*, taking in outside information about past situations like the one you're in.

[*]
Bayes, Thomas. 1702-1761 - English statistician and minister. The theorem which bears his name is a critical part of probability mathematics. He never published it himself, and so we have to thank his friend Richard Price for not losing this work to history.

Consider the headline "Violent Stabbings on the Rise." Without Bayesian thinking, you might become genuinely afraid because your chances of being a victim of assault or murder is higher than it was a few months ago. But a Bayesian approach will have you putting this information into the context of what you already know about violent crime.

You know that violent crime has been declining to its lowest rates in decades. Your city is safer now than it has been since this measurement started. Let's say your chance of being a victim of a stabbing last year was one in 10,000, or 0.01%. The article states, with accuracy, that violent crime has doubled. It is now two in 10,000, or 0.02%. Is that worth being terribly worried about? The prior information here is key. When we factor it in, we realize that our safety has not really been compromised.

Conversely, if we look at the diabetes statistics in the United States, our application of prior knowledge would lead us to a different conclusion. Here, a Bayesian analysis indicates you should be concerned. In 1958, 0.93% of the population was diagnosed with diabetes. In 2015 it was 7.4%. When you look at the intervening years, the climb in diabetes diagnosis is steady, not a spike. So the prior relevant data, or priors, indicate a trend that is worrisome.

It is important to remember that priors themselves are probability estimates. For each bit of prior knowledge, you are not putting it in a binary structure, saying it is true or not. You're assigning it a probability of being true. Therefore, you can't let your priors get in the way of processing new knowledge. In Bayesian terms, this is called the likelihood ratio or the Bayes factor. Any new information you encounter that challenges a prior simply means that the probability of that prior being true may be reduced. Eventually some priors are replaced completely. This is an ongoing cycle of challenging and validating what you believe you know. When making uncertain decisions, it's nearly always a mistake not to ask: What are the relevant priors? What might I already know that I can use to better understand the reality of the situation?

— Sidebar: Conditional Probability

Conditional Probability

Conditional probability is similar to Bayesian thinking in practice, but comes at it from a different angle. When you use historical events to predict the future, you have to be mindful of the conditions that surrounded that event.

Events can be independent, like tossing a coin, or dependent. In the latter case, it means the outcomes of an event are conditional on what preceded them. Let's say the last three times I've hung out with you and we've gone for ice cream, I've picked vanilla. Do you conclude that vanilla is my favorite, and thus I will always choose it? You want to check first if my choosing vanilla is independent or dependent. Am I the first to choose from 100 flavors? Or am I further down the line, when chocolate is no longer available?

My ice cream choice is independent if all the flavors are available each time someone in my group makes a choice. It is dependent if the preceding choices of my friends reduce what is available to me. In this case, the probability of my choosing vanilla is conditional on what is left after my friends make their choices.

Thus, using conditional probability means being very careful to observe the conditions preceding an event you'd like to understand.

Now we need to look at fat-tailed curves: Many of us are familiar with the bell curve, that nice, symmetrical wave that captures the relative frequency of so many things from height to exam scores. The bell curve is great because it's easy to understand and easy to use. Its technical name is "normal distribution." If we know we are in a bell curve situation, we can quickly identify our parameters and plan for the most likely outcomes.

Fat-tailed curves are different. Take a look.

At first glance they seem similar enough. Common outcomes cluster together, creating a wave. The difference is in the tails. In a bell curve the extremes are predictable. There can only be so much deviation from the mean. In a fat-tailed curve there is no real cap on extreme events.

The more extreme events that are possible, the longer the tails of the curve get. Any one extreme event is still unlikely, but the sheer number of options means that we can't rely on the most common outcomes as representing the average. The more extreme events that are possible, the higher the probability that one of them will occur. Crazy things are definitely going to happen, and we have no way of identifying when. — Sidebar: Orders of Magnitude

Think of it this way. In a bell curve type of situation, like displaying the distribution of height or weight in a human population, there are outliers on the spectrum of possibility, but the outliers have a fairly well-defined scope. You'll never meet a man who is ten times the size of an average man. But in a curve with fat tails, like wealth, the central tendency does not work the same way. You may regularly meet people who are ten, 100, or 10,000 times wealthier than the average person. That is a very different type of world.

Let's re-approach the example of the risks of violence we discussed in relation to Bayesian thinking. Suppose you hear that you had a greater risk of slipping on the stairs and

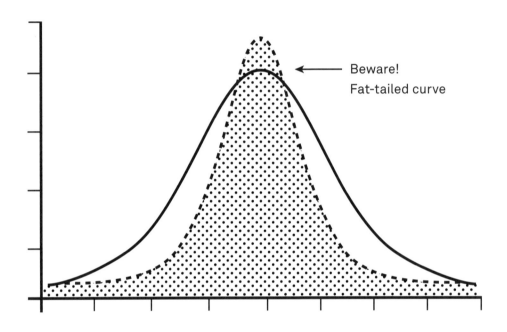

Beware!
Fat-tailed curve

Always be extra mindful of the tails:
They might mean everything.

1
Bernstein, Peter L.
Against the Gods: The Remarkable Story of Risk. New York: John Wiley and Sons, 1996. (This book includes an excellent discussion in Chapter 13 on the idea of the scope of events in the past as relevant to figuring out the probability of events in the future, drawing on the work of Frank Knight and John Maynard Keynes.)

cracking your head open than being killed by a terrorist. The statistics, the priors, seem to back it up: 1,000 people slipped on the stairs and died last year in your country and only 500 died of terrorism. Should you be more worried about stairs or terror events?

Some use examples like these to prove that terror risk is low—since the recent past shows very few deaths, why worry?[1] The problem is in the fat tails: The risk of terror violence is more like wealth, while stair-slipping deaths are more like height and weight. In the next ten years, how many events are possible? How fat is the tail?

The important thing is not to sit down and imagine every possible scenario in the tail (by definition, it is impossible) but to deal with fat-tailed domains in the correct way: by positioning ourselves to survive or even benefit from the wildly unpredictable future, by being the only ones thinking correctly and planning for a world we don't fully understand.

— Sidebar: Anti-fragility

Asymmetries: Finally, you need to think about something we might call "metaprobability"—the probability that your probability estimates themselves are any good.

This massively misunderstood concept has to do with asymmetries. If you look at nicely polished stock pitches made by professional investors, nearly every time an idea is presented, the investor looks their audience in the eye and states they think they're going to achieve a rate of return of 20% to 40% per annum, if not higher. Yet exceedingly few of them ever attain that mark, and it's not because they don't have any winners. It's because they get so many so wrong. They consistently overestimate their confidence in their probabilistic estimates. (For reference, the general stock market has returned no more than 7% to 8% per annum in the United States over a long period, before fees.)

Orders of Magnitude

Nassim Taleb puts his finger in the right place when he points out our *naive* use of probabilities. In *The Black Swan*, he argues that any small error in measuring the risk of an extreme event can mean we're not just slightly off, but way off—off by orders of magnitude, in fact. In other words, not just 10% wrong but ten times wrong, or 100 times wrong, or 1,000 times wrong. Something we thought could only happen every 1,000 years might be likely to happen in any given year! This is using false prior information and results in us underestimating the probability of the future distribution being different.

Taleb, Nassim.
The Black Swan: The Impact of the Highly Improbable, 2nd edition.
New York: Random House, 2010.

Anti-fragility

How do we benefit from the uncertainty of a world we don't understand, one dominated by "fat tails"? The answer to this was provided by Nassim Taleb in a book curiously titled *Antifragile*.

Here is the core of the idea. We can think about three categories of objects: Ones that are *harmed* by volatility and unpredictability, ones that are *neutral* to volatility and unpredictability, and finally, ones that *benefit* from it. The latter category is antifragile—like a package that wants to be mishandled. Up to a point, certain things benefit from volatility, and that's how we want to be. Why? Because the world is fundamentally unpredictable and volatile, and large events—panics, crashes, wars, bubbles, and so on—tend to have a disproportionate impact on outcomes.

There are two ways to handle such a world: try to predict, or try to prepare. Prediction is tempting. For all of human history, seers and soothsayers have turned a comfortable trade. The problem is that nearly all studies of "expert" predictions in such complex real-world realms as the stock market, geopolitics, and global finance have proven again and again that, for the rare and impactful events in our world, predicting is impossible! It's more efficient to prepare.

What are some ways we can prepare—arm ourselves with antifragility—so we can benefit from the volatility of the world?

The first one is what Wall Street traders would call "upside optionality", that is, seeking out situations that we expect have good odds of offering us opportunities. Take the example of attending a cocktail party where a lot of people you might like to know are in attendance. While nothing is *guaranteed* to happen—you may not meet those people, and if you do, it may not go well— you give yourself the benefit of serendipity and randomness. The worst thing that can happen is...nothing. One thing you know for sure is that you'll never meet them sitting at home. By going to the party, you improve your odds of encountering opportunity.

The second thing we can do is to learn how to fail properly. Failing properly has two major components. First, never take a risk that will do you in completely. (Never get taken out of the game completely.) Second, develop the personal resilience to *learn* from your failures and start again. With these two rules, you can only fail temporarily.

No one likes to fail. It hurts. But failure carries with it one huge antifragile gift: learning. Those who are not afraid to fail (properly) have a huge advantage over the rest. What they learn makes them less vulnerable to the volatility of the world. They benefit from it, in true antifragile fashion.

Let's say you'd like to start a successful business, but you have no business experience. Do you attend business school or start a business that might fail? Business school has its benefits, but business itself—the rough, jagged real-world experience of it—teaches through rapid feedback loops of success and failure. In other words, trial and error carries the precious commodity of information.

The *Antifragile* mindset is a unique one. Whenever possible, try to create scenarios where randomness and uncertainty are your friends, not your enemies.

–
Taleb, Nassim.
Antifragile. New York: Random House, 2012.

—
The SOE's primary goal in France was to coordinate and initiate sabotage and other subversive activities against the Germans.

Atkins, Vera.
1908-2000 - Romanian-British
intelligence officer. She received
high honors from both the British
and French governments for her
work for the allies during World
War II.

1
Helm, Sarah.
*A Life in Secrets: The Story of Vera
Atkins and the Lost Agents of SOE*.
London: Abacus, 2005.

Another common asymmetry is people's ability to estimate the effect of traffic on travel time. How often do you leave "on time" and arrive 20% early? Almost never? How often do you leave "on time" and arrive 20% late? All the time? Exactly. Your estimation errors are asymmetric, skewing in a single direction. This is often the case with probabilistic decision-making.

Far more probability estimates are wrong on the "over-optimistic" side than the "under-optimistic" side. You'll rarely read about an investor who aimed for 25% annual return rates who subsequently earned 40% over a long period of time. You can throw a dart at the Wall Street Journal and hit the names of lots of investors who aim for 25% per annum with each investment and end up closer to 10%.

The spy world

Successful spies are very good at probabilistic thinking. High-stakes survival situations tend to make us evaluate our environment with as little bias as possible.

When Vera Atkins* was second in command of the French unit of the Special Operations Executive (SOE), a British intelligence organization reporting directly to Winston Churchill during World War II[1], she had to make hundreds of decisions by figuring out the probable accuracy of inherently unreliable information.

Atkins was responsible for the recruitment and deployment of British agents into occupied France. She had to decide who could do the job, and where the best sources of intelligence were. These were literal life-and-death decisions, and all were based in probabilistic thinking.

First, how do you choose a spy? Not everyone can go undercover in high stress situations and make the contacts necessary to gather intelligence. The result of failure in France in WWII was not getting fired; it was death. What factors of personality and experience show that a person is right for the job?

la liberté pour la France . . . .
les libertés pour les Français

Many of the British Intelligence services worked with the French Resistance in WWII. It was a win-win. Expert knowledge of the territory for the British, weapons and financial support for the Resistance.

Even today, with advancements in psychology, interrogation, and polygraphs, it's still a judgment call.

For Vera Atkins in the 1940s, it was very much a process of assigning weight to the various factors and coming up with a probabilistic assessment of who had a decent chance of success. Who spoke French? Who had the confidence? Who was too tied to family? Who had the problem-solving capabilities? From recruitment to deployment, her development of each spy was a series of continually updated, educated estimates.

Getting an intelligence officer ready to go is only half the battle. Where do you send them? If your information was so great that you knew exactly where to go, you probably wouldn't need an intelligence mission. Choosing a target is another exercise in probabilistic thinking. You need to evaluate the reliability of the information you have and the networks you have set up. Intelligence is not evidence. There is no chain of command or guarantee of authenticity.

The stuff coming out of German-occupied France was at the level of grainy photographs, handwritten notes that passed through many hands on the way back to HQ, and unverifiable wireless messages sent quickly, sometimes sporadically, and with the operator under incredible stress. When deciding what to use, Atkins had to consider the relevancy, quality, and timeliness of the information she had.

She also had to make decisions based not only on what had happened, but what possibly could. Trying to prepare for every eventuality means that spies would never leave home, but they must somehow prepare for a good deal of the unexpected. After all, their jobs are often executed in highly volatile, dynamic environments. The women and men Atkins sent over to France worked in three primary occupations: organizers were responsible for recruiting locals, developing the network, and identifying sabotage targets; couriers moved information all around the country, connecting people and networks to coordinate activities; and wireless operators had to set up heavy communications equipment, disguise it, get information out of the country, and be ready to move at a moment's notice. All of these jobs were dangerous. The full scope of the threats was never completely identifiable. There were so many things that could go wrong, so many possibilities for discovery or betrayal, that it was impossible to plan for them all. The average life expectancy in France for one of Atkins's wireless operators was six weeks.

Finally, the numbers suggest an asymmetry in the estimation of the probability of success of each individual agent. Of the 400 agents that Atkins sent over to France, 100 were captured and killed. This is not meant to pass judgment on her skills or smarts. Probabilistic thinking can only get you in the ballpark. It doesn't guarantee 100% success.

There is no doubt that Atkins relied heavily on probabilistic thinking to guide her decisions in the challenging quest to disrupt German operations in France during World War II. It is hard to evaluate the success of an espionage career, because it is a job that comes with a lot of loss. Atkins was extremely successful in that her network conducted valuable sabotage to support the Allied cause during the war, but the loss of life was significant.

Conclusion

Successfully thinking in shades of probability means roughly identifying what matters, coming up with a sense of the odds, doing a check on our assumptions, and then making a decision. We can act with a higher level of certainty in complex, unpredictable situations. We can never know the future with exact precision. Probabilistic thinking is an extremely useful tool to evaluate how the world will most likely look so that we can effectively strategize.

Insurance Companies

The most probability-acute businesses in the world are insurance companies—because they must be. When we think of insurance, we might think of life insurance (the probability of a policyholder dying at a certain age), or auto insurance (the probability of being in a car accident), or maybe home insurance (the probability of a tree falling on the house). With the statistics available to us, the probabilities of these things are easy to price and predict across a large enough population.

But insurance is deeply wide-ranging, and insurers will insure almost any event, for a price. Insurance policies have been taken out on Victoria's Secret models' legs, on baseball players' arms, on the Pepsi Challenge and the NCAA tournament, and even on a famous country singer's breasts!

How is this possible? Only with a close attention to probability. What the great insurance companies in the world know how to do is pay attention to the important factors, even if they're not totally predictable, and price accordingly.

What is the probability of a Victoria's Secret model injuring her legs badly enough to end her career? One in 10,000? One in 100,000? Getting it right would mean evaluating her lifestyle, her habits, her health, her family history—and coming up with a price and a set of conditions that are good enough to provide a profit on average. It's not unlike handicapping a race at the horse tracks. You can always say yes to insuring, but the trick is to come up with the right price. And for that we need probability.

Causation vs. Correlation

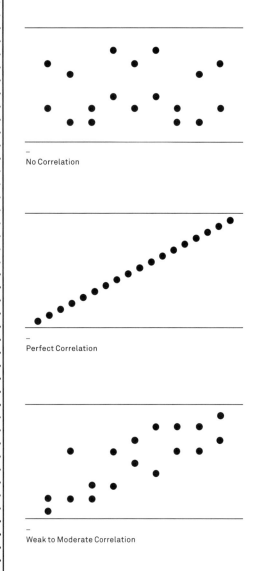

—
No Correlation

—
Perfect Correlation

—
Weak to Moderate Correlation

Confusion between these two terms often leads to a lot of inaccurate assumptions about the way the world works. We notice two things happening at the same time (correlation) and mistakenly conclude that one causes the other (causation). We then often act upon that erroneous conclusion, making decisions that can have immense influence across our lives. The problem is, without a good understanding of what is meant by these terms, these decisions fail to capitalize on real dynamics in the world and instead are successful only by luck.

No Correlation

The correlation coefficient between two measures, which varies between -1 and 1, is a measure of the relative weight of the factors they share. For example, two phenomena with few factors shared, such as bottled water consumption versus suicide rate, should have a correlation coefficient of close to 0. That is to say, if we looked at all countries in the world and plotted suicide rates of a specific year against per capita consumption of bottled water, the plot would show no pattern at all.

Perfect Correlation.

On the contrary, there are measures which are solely dependent on the same factor. A good example of this is temperature. The only factor governing temperature—velocity of molecules—is shared by all scales. Thus each degree in Celsius will have exactly one corresponding value in Fahrenheit. Therefore temperature in Celsius and Fahrenheit will have a correlation coefficient of 1 and the plot will be a straight line.

Weak to Moderate Correlation.

There are few phenomena in human sciences that have a correlation coefficient of 1. There are, however, plenty where the association is weak to moderate and there is some explanatory power between the two phenomena. Consider the correlation between height and weight, which would land somewhere between 0 and 1. While virtually every three-year-old will be lighter and shorter than every grown man, not all grown men or three-year-olds of the same height will weigh the same.

This variation and the corresponding lower degree of correlation implies that, while height is generally speaking a good predictor, there clearly are factors other than height at play.

In addition, correlation can sometimes work in reverse. Let's say you read a study that compares alcohol consumption rates in parents and their corresponding children's academic success. The study shows a relationship between high alcohol consumption and low academic success. Is this a causation or a correlation? It might be tempting to conclude a causation, such as the more parents drink, the worse their kids do in school.

However, this study has only demonstrated a relationship, not proved that one causes the other. The factors correlate—meaning that alcohol consumption in parents has an inverse relationship with academic success in children. It is entirely possible that having parents who consume a lot of alcohol leads to worse academic outcomes for their children. It is also possible, however, that the reverse is true, or even that having kids who do poorly in school causes parents to drink more. Trying to invert the relationship can help you sort through claims to determine if you are dealing with true causation or just correlation.

Causation

Whenever correlation is imperfect, extremes will soften over time. The best will always appear to get worse and the worst will appear to get better, regardless of any additional action. This is called regression to the mean, and it means we have to be extra careful when diagnosing causation. This is something that the general media and sometimes even trained scientists fail to recognize.

Consider the example Daniel Kahneman gives in *Thinking Fast and Slow:*[1]

Depressed children treated with an energy drink improve significantly over a three-month period. I made up this newspaper headline, but the fact it reports is true: if you treated a group of depressed children for some time with an energy drink, they

would show a clinically significant improvement. It is also the case that depressed children who spend some time standing on their head or hug a cat for twenty minutes a day will also show improvement.

Whenever coming across such headlines it is very tempting to jump to the conclusion that energy drinks, standing on the head, or hugging cats are all perfectly viable cures for depression. These cases, however, once again embody the regression to the mean:

Depressed children are an extreme group, they are more depressed than most other children—and extreme groups regress to the mean over time. The correlation between depression scores on successive occasions of testing is less than perfect, so there will be regression to the mean: depressed children will get somewhat better over time even if they hug no cats and drink no Red Bull.

We often mistakenly attribute a specific policy or treatment as the cause of an effect, when the change in the extreme groups would have happened anyway. This presents a fundamental problem: how can we know if the effects are real or simply due to variability?

Luckily there is a way to tell between a real improvement and something that would have happened anyway. That is the introduction of the so-called control group, which is expected to improve by regression alone. The aim of the research is to determine whether the treated group improves more than regression can explain.

In real life situations with the performance of specific individuals or teams, where the only real benchmark is the past performance and no control group can be introduced, the effects of regression can be difficult if not impossible to disentangle. We can compare against industry average, peers in the cohort group or historical rates of improvement, but none of these are perfect measures.

1
Kahneman, Daniel.
Thinking Fast and Slow. New York: Random House, 2011.

Inversion

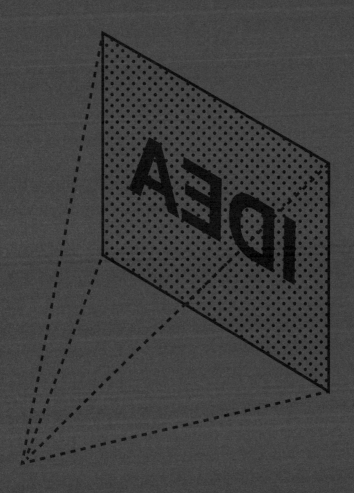

Change your perspective.

The test of a first-rate intelligence is the ability to hold two opposing ideas in mind at the same time and still retain the ability to function. One should, for example, be able to see that things are hopeless yet be determined to make them otherwise.

F. Scott Fitzgerald[1]

Inversion

Inversion is a powerful tool to improve your thinking because it helps you identify and remove obstacles to success. The root of inversion is "invert," which means to upend or turn upside down. As a thinking tool it means approaching a situation from the opposite end of the natural starting point. Most of us tend to think one way about a problem: forward. Inversion allows us to flip the problem around and think backward. Sometimes it's good to start at the beginning, but it can be more useful to start at the end.

Think of it this way: Avoiding stupidity is easier than seeking brilliance. Combining the ability to think forward and backward allows you to see reality from multiple angles.

There are two approaches to applying inversion in your life.

1.   Start by assuming that what you're trying to prove is either true or false, then show what else would have to be true.
2.   Instead of aiming directly for your goal, think deeply about what you want to *avoid* and then see what options are left over.

Set your assumptions: The 19th century German mathematician Carl Jacobi[*] became famous for a number of reasons—including solving some ungodly difficult problems—but is perhaps best remembered for his advice to "invert, always invert." Jacobi solved a range of problems by starting with the endpoint. When faced with proving an axiom in a difficult math problem, he might instead assume a property of the axiom was correct and then try to determine the consequences of this assumption. From that point, he could work out surprising, and at times counterintuitive, insights.

— Sidebar: The Most Successful Detective of All Time

[*]
Jacobi, Carl.
1804-1851 - German mathematician who made fundamental contributions to elliptic functions, dynamics, and number theory.

[1]
Fitzgerald, F. Scott.
"The Crack-up, Part I." *Esquire*, February 1936.

Jacobi was not the first mathematician to use inversion. In fact, inversion is a staple of mathematical, philosophical, and scientific inquiry. We can look around today and appreciate that we can't see atoms and quarks, but we know they exist because we can make predictions about their behavior and test those predictions.

Or we can go back 2,300 years and look at the work of the Greek Hippasus, a follower of Pythagoras.[1] (Yes, the one with the Theorem.) His attempts to derive the square root of 2, and his original direct approach to solving the problem (essentially, dividing larger and larger whole numbers into each other) were both fruitless and time consuming. He hit an impasse, realizing that he'd never be able to definitely solve the problem by thinking forward. In his increasing frustration, Hippasus decided to take the reverse route, thinking about what the square root of 2 might *imply*, and working backwards from there. If he couldn't find it the way he had expected to, he'd start by proving what the number *couldn't* be. His quest forever changed what we understood about mathematics, and led to the discovery of the first irrational number.

Mathematics is not the only area where using inversion can produce surprising and non-intuitive results. In the 1920s the American Tobacco Company wanted to sell more of their Lucky Strike cigarettes to women. Men were smoking, but women weren't. There were pervasive taboos against women smoking—it was seen as a man's activity. Women therefore presented an untapped market that had the potential of providing huge revenue. The head of the company thought that they needed to convince women that smoking would make them thinner, riding on the slimness trend that had already begun, so he hired Edward Bernays[*], who came up with a truly revolutionary marketing campaign.[2, 3]

In the style of the inversion approach described above, Bernays did not ask, "How do I sell more cigarettes to women?" Instead, he wondered, if women bought and smoked

[*] Bernays, Edward. 1891-1995 - Austrian-American. Known as "the Father of Public Relations". Although his influence cannot be doubted, his legacy is one of brilliant but sometimes unethical strategies that consumers and citizens are still navigating today.

[1] Heath, Thomas. *A History of Greek Mathematics, Volume 1, From Thales to Euclid.* UK: Oxford University Press, 1921.

[2] Axelrod, Alan. *Profiles in Folly: History's Worst Decisions and Why They Went Wrong.* New York: Sterling, 2008.

[3] Tye, Larry. *The Father of Spin.* New York: Holt and Company, 1998.

The Most Successful Detective of All Time

1
Doyle, Arthur Conan.
The Adventures of Sherlock Holmes.
London: George Newnes, 1892.

T he first great detective to capture the public imagination was Sherlock Holmes. He solved cases in ways that were unfathomable to others, yet seemed obvious in retrospect. He gave the appearance of being a magician, but really he was an excellent observer. He was also a master of inversion.

In his third case, "A Scandal in Bohemia,"[1] Holmes is hired by a king to recover a compromising photograph in which the king appears with an American opera singer, Irene Adler. The king is fearful that Adler will use the picture of the two of them to prevent his upcoming marriage or to blackmail him in the future. He does not want to live under this threat, and so hires Sherlock Holmes to retrieve the picture from Adler.

Presented with this task, what does Holmes do? What would you do? Does he study Adler for months to determine where, based on her personality, she is likely to hide the picture? Does he break into her house and perform a systematic exploration of every nook and cranny? No. Instead, he inverts the problem.

If it is true that Adler has this compromising picture of the king and is planning to blackmail him, what would also be true? Likely that she would greatly value the photo as it will bring her money, and that it would be hidden in an accessible location so she could retrieve it in a hurry. We tend to keep our most prized possessions where we can easily grab them in case of emergency.

So Holmes contrives a scenario in which he is able to be in her house while Watson creates an illusion of a fire on the street outside. Believing the threat, Adler takes the photo out of its hiding place before escaping. In one instant Holmes both confirms the existence of the photo and now knows its whereabouts. By starting with the logical outcome of his assumptions and seeking to validate those, he advances his case with significantly more efficiency and accuracy than if he had searched first for proof of the assumptions themselves.

Bernays never believed his own propaganda on smoking,
for years pressuring his wife to quit.

1, 2
Axelrod, Alan.
Ibid.

cigarettes, what else would have to be true? What would have to change in the world to make smoking desirable to women and socially acceptable? Then—a step farther—once he knew what needed to change, how would he achieve that?

To tackle the idea of smoking as a slimming aid, he mounted a large anti-sweets campaign. After dinner, it was about cigarettes, not dessert. Cigarettes were slimming, while desserts would ruin one's figure. But Bernays's real stroke of genius lay not just in coming out with adverts to convince women to stay slim by smoking cigarettes; "instead, he sought nothing less than to reshape American society and culture."[1] He solicited journalists and photographers to promote the virtues of being slim. He sought testimonials from doctors about the health value of smoking after a meal. He combined this approach with

> ...altering the very environment, striving to create a world in which the cigarette was ubiquitous. He mounted a campaign to persuade hotels and restaurants to add cigarettes to dessert-list menus, and he provided such magazines as House and Garden with feature articles that included menus designed to preserve readers 'from the dangers of overeating'.... The idea was not only to influence opinion but to remold life itself. Bernays approached designers, architects, and cabinetmakers in an effort to persuade them to design kitchen cabinets that included special compartments for cigarettes, and he spoke to the manufacturers of kitchen containers to add cigarette tins to their traditional lines of labeled containers for coffee, tea, sugar, and flour.[2]

The result was a complete shift in the consumption habits of American women. It wasn't just about selling the cigarette, it was reorganizing society to make cigarettes an inescapable part of the American woman's daily experience.

Bernays's efforts to make smoking in public socially acceptable had equally startling results. He linked cigarette smoking with women's emancipation. To smoke was to be free. Cigarettes were marketed as "torches of freedom." He orchestrated public events, including an infamous parade on Easter Sunday in 1929 which featured women smoking as they walked in the parade. He left no detail unattended, so public perception of smoking was changed almost overnight. He both normalized it and made it desirable in one swoop.

Although the campaign utilized more principles than just inversion, it was the original decision to invert the approach that provided the framework from which the campaign was created and executed. Bernays didn't focus on how to sell more cigarettes to women within the existing social structure. Sales would have undoubtedly been a lot more limited. Instead he thought about what the world would look like if women smoked often and anywhere, and then set about trying to make that world a reality. Once he did that, selling cigarettes to women was comparatively easy.

This inversion approach became a staple of Bernays's work. He used the descriptor "appeals of indirection", and each time when "hired to sell a product or service, he instead sold whole new ways of behaving, which appeared obscure but over time reaped huge rewards for his clients and redefined the very texture of American life."[1]

What are you trying to avoid? Instead of thinking through the achievement of a positive outcome, we could ask ourselves how we might achieve a terrible outcome, and let that guide our decision-making. Index funds are a great example of stock market inversion promoted and brought to bear by Vanguard's John Bogle.[2][*] Instead of asking how to beat the market, as so many before him, Bogle recognized the difficulty of the task. Everyone is trying to beat the market. No one is doing it with any consistency, and in the process real people are losing actual money. So he inverted the approach. The question then became, how can we help investors minimize losses to fees and poor money manager selection? The results were one of

[*]
Bogle, John.
1929 - American investor, business magnate, and philanthropist. He is the founder and retired chief executive of The Vanguard Group.

[1]
Tye, Larry.
The Father of Spin. New York: Holt and Company, 1998.

[2]
Bogle, John.
Common Sense on Mutual Funds: New Imperatives for the Intelligent Investor. USA: John Wiley and Sons, 1999.

Lewin, Kurt.
1890-1947 - German-American psychologist. Often recognized as the founder of social psychology, he was one of the first to study group dynamics and organizational development.

1
Lewin's original work on force field analysis can be found in Lewin, Kurt. *Field Theory in Social Science.* New York: Harper and Row, 1951.

the greatest ideas—index funds—and one of the greatest powerhouse firms in the history of finance.

The index fund operates on the idea that accruing wealth has a lot to do with minimizing loss. Think about your personal finances. Often we focus on positive goals, such as "I want to be rich," and use this to guide our approach. We make investing and career choices based on our desire to accumulate wealth. We chase after magical solutions, like attempting to outsmart the stock market. These inevitably get us nowhere, and we have usually taken some terrible risks in the process which actually leave us worse off.

Instead, we can try inverting the goal. It becomes, not getting rich, but avoiding being poor. Instead of trying to divine the decisions that will bring wealth, we first try to eliminate those behaviors that are guaranteed to erode it. There are some pretty obvious ones. Spending more than we make, paying high interest rates on debt so that we can't tackle paying back the principal, and not starting to save as early as we can to take advantage of the power of compounding, are all concrete financial behaviors that cost us money. We can more readily secure wealth by using inversion to make sure we are not doing the worst things that prevent the accumulation of wealth. — Sidebar: Inversion Leads to Innovation

One of the theoretical foundations for this type of thinking comes from psychologist Kurt Lewin.[1][*] In the 1930s he came up with the idea of force field analysis, which essentially recognizes that in any situation where change is desired, successful management of that change requires applied inversion. Here is a brief explanation of his process:
1. Identify the problem
2. Define your objective
3. Identify the forces that support change towards your objective
4. Identify the forces that impede change towards the objective

5.   Strategize a solution! This may involve both augmenting or adding to the forces in step 3, and reducing or eliminating the forces in step 4.

Even if we are quite logical, most of us stop after step 3. Once we figure out our objective, we focus on the things we need to put in place to make it happen, the new training or education, the messaging and marketing. But Lewin theorized that it can be just as powerful to remove obstacles to change.

The inversion happens between steps 3 and 4. Whatever angle you choose to approach your problem from, you need to then follow with consideration of the opposite angle. Think about not only what you could do to solve a problem, but what you could do to make it worse—and then avoid doing that, or eliminate the conditions that perpetuate it.

«He wins his battles by making no mistakes.»

Sun Tzu [1]

This inversion approach was used by Florence Nightingale* to help significantly reduce the mortality rate of British soldiers in military hospitals in the late 19th century. She is often remembered as the founder of modern nursing, but she was also an excellent statistician and was the first woman elected to the Royal Statistical Society in 1858.

During the first winter of the Crimean War, 1854–55, the British Army endured a death rate of 23%. The next winter that rate had dropped to 2.5%.[2] The main reason for the change was a much better understanding of what was actually killing the soldiers, an understanding that rested on the detailed statistics that Florence Nightingale started to collect. She demonstrated that the leading cause of death by far was poor sanitation. In her famous polar-area chart, a completely new way of presenting data at the time, she captured a visual representation of the statistics that made them easy to understand.

[1]
 Sun Tzu.
Ibid.

*
Nightingale, Florence.
1820-1910 - English social reformer, statistician, and the founder of modern nursing. By turning nursing into a profession and collecting detailed statistics on hospital conditions, she improved the lives of people all over the world.

[2]
McDonald, Lynn.
"Florence Nightingale, statistics, and the Crimean War." *Journal of the Royal Statistical Society: Series A* (2014) 177, Part 3, pp. 569–586

Inversion Leads to Innovation

Using inversion to identify your end goal and work backward from there can lead to innovation. If you had to make a guess on who invented closed circuit television (CCTV) in the United States, whom would you choose? A large institution like the Department of Defense? A telecom company? Some techie in a police department? You probably wouldn't name the late Marie Van Brittan Brown, who, along with her husband Albert Brown, filed the first patent for a closed circuit monitoring system in 1966. She was a nurse, living in the Jamaica neighborhood of Queens, New York, and as such worked irregular hours. When she was home alone, she felt unsafe. In an interesting example of inversion, she decided to do something about it.

In the same situation, most of us would work forward, thinking of safety-oriented additions we can make to our existing set-up, like more locks, or having a friend stay over. Van Brittan Brown, however, went a step further, asking what would need to change in order for her to feel safer. She identified that it was her inability to see and communicate with persons outside her door that made her feel the most vulnerable when home alone. Working backward, her thinking may have gone something like this: what can I do to change that situation? What would have to be in place? Van Brittan Brown followed this through, and CCTV was born.

Van Brittan Brown and her husband designed a camera system that would move between four holes in the door, feeding the images to a TV monitor set up in the home. The images would allow her to get a complete view of who was at the door, and additional technology allowed for communication with the person outside without the door being opened. Further, they developed a feature that would allow her to either let the person in, or sound an alarm to notify a neighbor or watchman.

To be fair, we will likely never know the thought process that led Van Brittan Brown to develop and patent this technology, but her story demonstrates that working backward from a goal can spur the innovation to reach it.

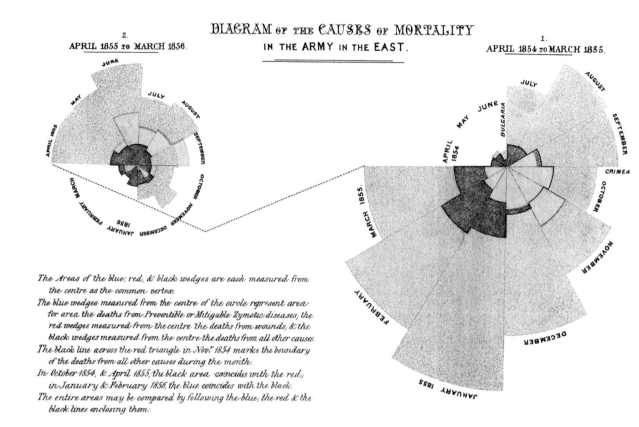

DIAGRAM OF THE CAUSES OF MORTALITY
IN THE ARMY IN THE EAST.

2.
APRIL 1855 TO MARCH 1856.

1.
APRIL 1854 TO MARCH 1855.

The Areas of the blue, red, & black wedges are each measured from
the centre as the common vertex.

The blue wedges measured from the centre of the circle represent area
for area the deaths from Preventible or Mitigable Zymotic diseases, the
red wedges measured from the centre the deaths from wounds, & the
black wedges measured from the centre the deaths from all other causes.

The black line across the red triangle in Nov.r 1854 marks the boundary
of the deaths from all other causes during the month.

In October 1854, & April 1855, the black area coincides with the red;
in January & February 1856, the blue coincides with the black.

The entire areas may be compared by following the blue, the red & the
black lines enclosing them.

Nightingale's use of statistics helped to identify the real
problem of army hospital deaths.

1
McDonald, Lynn.
Ibid.

2
Kopf, Edwin W.
"Florence Nightingale as Statisti-
cian." *Publications of the American
Statistical Association*. Vol. 15, No.
116 (Dec., 1916), pp. 388-404

3
Sun Tzu.
Ibid.

Improve the sanitary conditions in the hospitals, she explained, and many soldiers' lives will be saved.

Nightingale's use of statistics helped to identify the real problem of army hospital deaths. She was able to demonstrate not only what the army could do to improve outcomes, but, just as important, what they had to avoid doing to stop making things worse. She reflected on the knowledge that could be derived from statistics and, in another instance of inversion thinking, she advocated for their use as a means of prevention.[1] It became not so much "how do we fix this problem," but "how do we stop it from happening in the first place." She took the knowledge and experience she gained in the Crimea and began gathering statistics not just for British Army field hospitals, but for domestic ones as well. She demonstrated that unsanitary conditions in military hospitals were a real problem causing many preventable deaths.[2]

Nightingale's advocacy for statistics ultimately went much further than British military hospitals. But her use of statistics to improve sanitary conditions can be seen as an example of applied inversion. She used them to advocate for both solving problems and the invert, preventing them.

«Hence to fight and conquer in all your battles is not supreme excellence; supreme excellence consists in breaking the enemy's resistance without fighting.»

Sun Tzu [3]

Conclusion

Inversion shows us that we don't always need to be geniuses, nor do we need to limit its application to mathematical and scientific proofs. Simply invert, always invert, when you are stuck. If you take the results of your inversion seriously, you might make a great deal of progress on solving your problems.

Occam's Razor

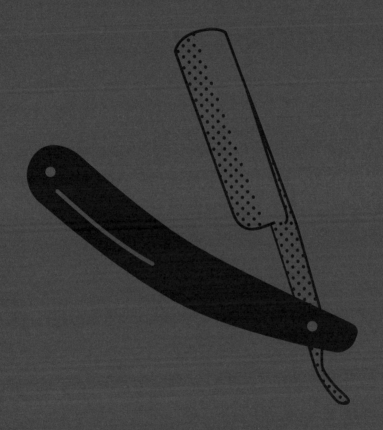

Keep it simple.

Anybody can make the simple complicated. Creativity is making the complicated simple.

Charles Mingus[1]

Occam's Razor

Simpler explanations are more likely to be true than complicated ones. This is the essence of Occam's Razor, a classic principle of logic and problem-solving. Instead of wasting your time trying to disprove complex scenarios, you can make decisions more confidently by basing them on the explanation that has the fewest moving parts.

We all jump to overly complex explanations about something. Husband late getting home? What if he's been in a car accident? Son grew a centimeter less than he did last year? What if there is something wrong with him? Your toe hurts? What if you have bone cancer? Although it is possible that any of these worst case scenarios could be true, without any other correlating factors, it is significantly more likely that your husband got caught up at work, you mismeasured your son, and your shoe is too tight.

We often spend lots of time coming up with very complicated narratives to explain what we see around us. From the behavior of people on the street to physical phenomena, we get caught up in assuming vast icebergs of meaning beyond the tips that we observe. This is a common human tendency, and it serves us well in some situations, such as creating art. However, complexity takes work to unravel, manage, and understand. Occam's Razor is a great tool for avoiding unnecessary complexity by helping you identify and commit to the simplest explanation possible.

Named after the medieval logician William of Ockham[*], Occam's Razor is a general rule by which we select among competing explanations. Ockham wrote that "a plurality is not to be posited without necessity"—essentially that we should prefer the simplest explanation with the fewest moving parts.[2,3] They are easier to falsify, easier to understand, and generally more likely to be correct. Occam's Razor is not an iron law but a

1
Mingus, Charles.
Charles Mingus - More Than a Fake Book. Hal Leonard Corporation, 1991.

*
William of Ockham.
1285-1347 - English philosopher and theologian. He is considered to be one of the major figures of medieval thought, and contributed to many branches of philosophy, like logic and ethics, as well as theology.

2
Franklin, James.
The Science of Conjecture: Evidence and Probability before Pascal. Baltimore: The Johns Hopkins University Press, 2001.

3
Maurer, Armand.
"Ockham's Razor and Chatton's Anti-Razor." *Mediaeval Studies*, volume 46, pp. 463-475.

tendency and a mind-frame you can choose to use: If all else is equal, that is if two competing models both have equal explanatory power, it's more likely that the simple solution suffices.

Of course, it's unlikely that Ockham himself derived the idea. It had been in use since antiquity. Nor was Ockham the last to note the value of simplicity. The principle was stated in another useful way by the 18th-century Scottish philosopher David Hume*, in his famous *Enquiry Concerning Human Understanding.* Writing about the truth or untruth of miracles, Hume stated that we should default to skepticism about them.[1]

Why? It wasn't simply that Hume was a buzzkill. He had a specific, Occam-like reason for being cautious about miracles. By definition, a miracle is something which has happened outside of our normal understanding of the way nature works. If the miracle was not outside of our common experience, we wouldn't consider its occurrence miraculous. If there was a simple explanation for the occurrence based on mostly common knowledge, we likely wouldn't pay much attention to it at all.

Therefore, the most simple explanation for a miracle is that the miracle-witnesser is not describing the event correctly, or the miracle represents a more common phenomenon that we currently don't properly understand. As scientist and writer Carl Sagan* explains in *The Demon Haunted World*,

> A multitude of aspects of the natural world that were considered miraculous only a few generations ago are now thoroughly understood in terms of physics and chemistry. At least some of the mysteries of today will be comprehensively solved by our descendants. The fact that we cannot now produce a detailed understanding of, say, altered states of consciousness in terms of brain chemistry no more implies the existence of a 'spirit world' than a sunflower following the Sun in its course across the sky was evidence of a literal miracle before we knew about phototropism and plant hormones.[2]

*
Hume, David.
1711-1776 - Scottish philosopher, historian and economist. Best known today for his influential system of philosophical empiricism, skepticism and naturalism, resting on the idea that all human knowledge is founded solely in experience.

*
Sagan, Carl.
1934-1996 - American astronomer, astrophysicist, and great communicator of science. He assembled the first physical messages sent into space. He also narrated and co-wrote *Cosmos: A Personal Voyage*, the most widely watched series in the history of American Public television.

1
Hume, David.
An Enquiry Concerning Human Understanding and Other Writings. New York: Cambridge University Press, 2007.

2
Sagan, Carl.
The Demon Haunted World. New York: Random House, 1995.

Rubin, Vera.
1928-2016 - American astronomer.
She received multiple honors for
her achievements in astronomy,
and spent her life advocating for
and mentoring women in science.

3
Scoles, Sarah.
"How Vera Rubin confirmed dark
matter." Astronomy.com, October 4,
2016. Retrieved from: http://www.
astronomy.com/news/2016/10/
vera-rubin

4
Larsen, Kristine.
"Vera Cooper Rubin." *Jewish
Women: A Comprehensive Historical
Encyclopedia*. 1 March 2009. Jewish
Women's Archive. Retrieved from:
https://jwa.org/encyclopedia/
article/rubin-vera-cooper

5
Panek, Richard.
"Vera Rubin Didn't Discover Dark
Matter." *Scientific American*,
December 29, 2016. Retrieved from:
https://blogs.scientificamerican.
com/guest-blog/vera-rubin-did-
nt-discover-dark-matter/

The simpler explanation for a miracle is that there are principles of nature being exploited that we do not understand. This is Hume's and Sagan's point.

Dark what?

In the mid-1970s astronomer Vera Rubin[*] had a very interesting problem. She had a bunch of data about the behavior of galaxies piling up that wasn't explained by contemporary theories.[3,4,5]

Rubin had been observing the behavior of the Andromeda Galaxy, and had noticed something very strange. As explained in an article on Astronomy.com, "the vast spiral seemed to be rotating all wrong. The stuff at the edges was moving just as fast as the stuff near the center, apparently violating Newton's Laws of Motion (which also govern how the planets move around our Sun)." This didn't make any sense. Gravity should exert less pull on distant objects, which should move slower. But Rubin was observing something entirely different.

One possible explanation was something that had been theorized as far back as 1933, by Swiss astrophysicist Fritz Zwicky, who coined the phrase "dark matter" to describe a mass we couldn't see, but which was influencing the behavior of the orbits in the galaxies. Dark matter became the simplest explanation for the observed phenomenon, and Vera Rubin has been credited with providing the first evidence of its existence. What is particularly interesting is that to this day no one has ever actually discovered dark matter.

Why are more complicated explanations less likely to be true? Let's work it out mathematically. Take two competing explanations, each of which seem to equally explain a given phenomenon. If one of them requires the interaction of three variables and the other the interaction of thirty variables, all of which *must* have occurred to arrive at the stated conclusion, which of these is more likely to be in error? If each variable has

—
It was Rubin's observations of the Andromeda galaxy that led to her to collect the first evidence in support of the theory of dark matter—a substance that does not emit energy or light.

1
Randall, Lisa.
Dark Matter and the Dinosaurs.
New York: HarperCollins, 2015.

2
Sagan, Carl.
Ibid.

a 99% chance of being correct, the first explanation is only 3% likely to be wrong. The second, more complex explanation, is about nine times as likely to be wrong, or 26%. The simpler explanation is more robust in the face of uncertainty.

Dark matter is an excellent theory with a lot of explanatory power. As Lisa Randall explains in *Dark Matter and the Dinosaurs*, measurements of dark matter so far fit in exactly with what we understand about the Universe. Although we can't see it, we can make predictions based on our understanding of it, and test those predictions. She writes, "It would be even more mysterious to me if the matter we can see with our eyes is all the matter that exists."[1] Dark matter is currently the simplest explanation for certain phenomena we observe in the Universe. The great thing about science, however, is that it continually seeks to validate its assumptions.

Sagan wrote that "extraordinary claims require extraordinary proof."[2] He dedicated much ink to a rational investigation of extraordinary claims. He felt most, or nearly all, were susceptible to simpler and more parsimonious explanations. UFOs, paranormal activity, telepathy, and a hundred other seemingly mystifying occurrences could be better explained with a few simple real world variables. And as Hume suggested, if they couldn't, it was a lot more likely that we needed to update our understanding of the world than that a miracle had occurred.

And so, dark matter remains, right now, the simplest explanation for the peculiar behavior of galaxies. Scientists, however, continue to try to conclusively discover dark matter and thus try to determine if our understanding of the world is correct. If dark matter eventually becomes too complicated an explanation, it could be that the data describes something we don't yet understand about the universe. We can then apply Occam's Razor to update to what is the simplest, and thus easiest to verify, explanation. Vera Rubin herself, after noting that scientists always felt like they were ten years away from

99% chance of being correct

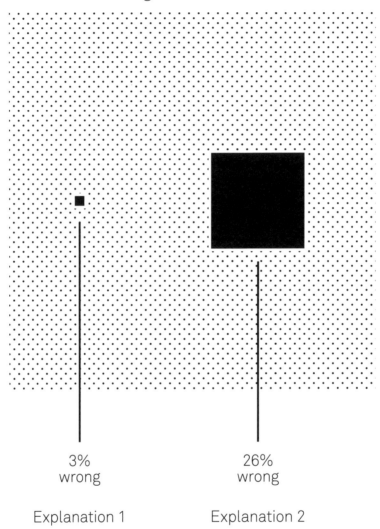

3%
wrong

26%
wrong

Explanation 1

Explanation 2

1
Panek, Richard.
Ibid.

2
Vara-Orta, Francisco.
"A reservoir goes undercover: The
DWP dumps about 400,000 black
balls into the water to block forma-
tion of the carcinogen bromate."
Los Angeles Times, June 10, 2008.

discovering dark matter without ever closing the gap, was described in an interview as thinking, "The longer that dark matter went undetected, … the more likely she thought the solution to the mystery would be a modification to our understanding of gravity."[1] This claim, demanding a total overhaul of our established theories of gravity, would correspondingly require extraordinary proof!

Simplicity can increase efficiency

With limited time and resources, it is not possible to track down every theory with a plausible explanation of a complex, uncertain event. Without the filter of Occam's Razor, we are stuck chasing down dead ends. We waste time, resources, and energy.

The great thing about simplicity is that it can be so powerful. Sometimes unnecessary complexity just papers over the systemic flaws that will eventually choke us. Opting for the simple helps us make decisions based on how things really are. Here are two short examples of those who got waylaid chasing down complicated solutions when simple ones were most effective.

The ten-acre Ivanhoe Reservoir in Los Angeles provides drinking water for over 600,000 people. Its nearly 60 million gallons of water are disinfected with chlorine, as is common practice.[2] Ground water often contains elevated levels of a chemical called bromide. When chlorine and bromide mix, then are exposed to sunlight, they create a dangerous carcinogen called bromate.

In order to avoid poisoning the water supply, the L.A. Department of Water and Power (DWP) needed a way to shade the water's surface. Brainstorming sessions had yielded only two infeasible solutions, building either a ten-acre tarp or a huge retractable dome over the reservoir. Then a DWP biologist suggested using "bird balls," the floating balls that airports use to keep birds from congregating near runways. They require

Occam's Razor in the Medical Field

Occam's Razor can be quite powerful in the medical field, for both doctors and patients. Let's suppose that a patient shows up at a doctor's office with horrible flu-like symptoms. Are they more likely to have the flu or have contracted Ebola?

This is a problem best solved by a concept we explored in the chapter on Probabilistic Thinking, called Bayesian Updating. It's a way of using general background knowledge in solving specific problems with new information. We know that generally the flu is far more common than Ebola, so when a good doctor encounters a patient with what looks like the flu, the simplest explanation is almost certainly the correct one. A diagnosis of Ebola means a call to the Center for Disease Control and a quarantine—an expensive and panic-inducing mistake if the patient just has the flu. Thus, medical students are taught to heed the saying, "When you hear hoofbeats, think horses, not zebras."

And for patients, Occam's Razor is a good counter to hypochondria. Based on the same principles, you factor in the current state of your health to an evaluation of your current symptoms. Knowing that the simplest explanation is most likely to be true can help us avoid unnecessary panic and stress.

3
Simons, Marlise.
"Face Masks Fool the Bengal
Tigers." *The New York Times*,
September 5, 1989.

no construction, no parts, no labor, no maintenance, and cost US$0.40 each. Three million UV-deflecting black balls were then deployed in Ivanhoe and other LA reservoirs, a simple solution to a potentially serious problem.

In another life-and-death situation, in 1989 Bengal tigers killed about 60 villagers from India's Ganges delta.[1] No weapons seemed to work against them, including lacing dummies with live wires to shock the tigers away from human populations.

Then a student at the Science Club of Calcutta noticed that tigers only attacked when they thought they were unseen, and recalled that the patterns decorating some species of butterflies, beetles, and caterpillars look like big eyes, ostensibly to trick predators into thinking their prey was also watching them. The result: a human face mask, worn on the back of head. Remarkably, no one wearing a mask was attacked by a tiger for the next three years; anyone killed by tigers during that time had either refused to wear the mask, or had taken it off while working. — Sidebar: Occam's Razor in the Medical Field

A few caveats

One important counter to Occam's Razor is the difficult truth that some things are simply not that simple. The regular recurrence of fraudulent human organizations like pyramid schemes and Ponzi schemes is not a miracle, but neither is it obvious. No simple explanation suffices, exactly. They are a result of a complex set of behaviors, some happening almost by accident or luck, and some carefully designed with the intent to deceive. It isn't a bit easy to spot the development of a fraud. If it was, they'd be stamped out early. Yet, to this day, frauds frequently grow to epic proportions before they are discovered.

Alternatively, consider the achievement of human flight. It, too, might seem like a miracle to our 17th century friar, but it isn't—it's a natural consequence of applied physics. Still, it took a long time for humans to figure out because it's not

The Razor in Leadership

When Louis Gerstner took over IBM in the early 1990s, during one of the worst periods of struggle in its history, many business pundits called for a statement of his vision. What rabbit would Gerstner pull out of his hat to save Big Blue?

It seemed a logical enough demand—wouldn't a technology company that had fallen behind need a grand vision of brilliant technological leadership to regain its place among the leaders of American innovation? As Gerstner put it, "The IBM organization, so full of brilliant, insightful people, would have loved to receive a bold recipe for success—the more sophisticated, the more complicated the recipe, the better everyone would have liked it."

Smartly, Gerstner realized that the simple approach was most likely to be the effective one. His famous reply was that "the last thing IBM needs right now is a vision." What IBM actually needed to do was to serve its customers, compete for business in the here and now, and focus on businesses that were already profitable. It needed simple, tough-minded business execution.

By the end of the 1990s, Gerstner had provided exactly that, bringing IBM back from the brink without any brilliant visions or massive technological overhauls.

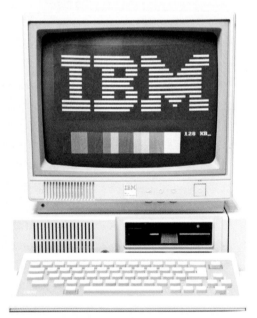

Gerstner, Louis V.
Who Says Elephants Can't Dance? Leading a Great Enterprise Through Dramatic Change. New York: HarperCollins, 2003.

168 / 169Occam's Razor

simple at all. In fact, the invention of powered human flight is highly counterintuitive, requiring an understanding of airflow, lift, drag, and combustion, among other difficult concepts. Only a precise combination of the right factors will do. You can't just know enough to get the aircraft off the ground, you need to keep it in the air!

Simple as we wish things were, irreducible complexity, like simplicity, is a part of our reality. Therefore, we can't use this Razor to create artificial simplicity. If something cannot be broken down any further, we must deal with it as it is.

How do you know something is as simple as it can be? Think of computer code. Code can sometimes be excessively complex. In trying to simplify it, we would still have to make sure it can perform the functions we need it to. This is one way to understand simplicity. An explanation can be simplified only to the extent that it can still provide an accurate understanding.

Conclusion

Of course, focusing on simplicity when all others are focused on complexity is a hallmark of genius, and it's easier said than done. But always remembering that a simpler explanation is more likely to be correct than a complicated one goes a long way towards helping us conserve our most precious resources of time and energy. — Sidebar: The Razor in Leadership

Hanlon's Razor

Don't assume the worst.

I need to listen
well so that I hear
what is not said.

Thuli Madonsela[1]

Hanlon's Razor

Hard to trace in its origin, Hanlon's Razor states that we should not attribute to malice that which is more easily explained by stupidity. In a complex world, using this model helps us avoid paranoia and ideology. By not generally assuming that bad results are the fault of a bad actor, we look for options instead of missing opportunities. This model reminds us that people do make mistakes. It demands that we ask if there is another reasonable explanation for the events that have occurred. The explanation most likely to be right is the one that contains the least amount of intent.

Assuming the worst intent crops up all over our lives. Consider road rage, a growing problem in a world that is becoming short on patience and time. When someone cuts you off, to assume malice is to assume the other person has done a lot of risky work. In order for someone to deliberately get in your way they have to notice you, gauge the speed of your car, consider where you are headed, and swerve in at exactly the right time to cause you to slam on the brakes, yet not cause an accident. That is some effort. The simpler and thus more likely explanation is that they didn't see you. It was a mistake. There was no intent. So why would you assume the former? Why do our minds make these kinds of connections when the logic says otherwise?

The famous Linda problem, demonstrated by the psychologists Daniel Kahneman[2] and Amos Tversky in a 1982 paper, is an illuminating example of how our minds work and why we need Hanlon's Razor. It went like this:

Linda is 31 years old, single, outspoken, and very bright. She majored in philosophy. As a student, she was deeply concerned with issues of discrimination and social justice, and also participated in anti-nuclear demonstrations.

1
Madonsela, Thuli.
Quoted in "Thuli Madonsela: SA's Iron Lady." Corruption Watch, March 8, 2013. Retrieved from: http://www.corruptionwatch.org.za/thuli-madonsela-sas-iron-lady

2
Kahneman, Daniel.
Thinking Fast and Slow. New York: Random House, 2011.

Which is more probable?

1. Linda is a bank teller.
2. Linda is a bank teller and is active in the feminist movement.

The majority of respondents chose option 2. Why? The wording used to describe her suggests Linda is feminist. But Linda could only be a bank teller, or a feminist *and* a bank teller. So naturally the majority of students concluded she was both. They didn't know anything about what she did, but because they were led to believe she had to be a feminist they couldn't reject that option, even though the math of statistics makes it more likely that a single condition is true instead of multiple conditions. In other words, every feminist bank teller is a bank teller, but not every bank teller is a feminist.

Thus, Kahneman and Tversky showed that students would, with enough vivid wording, assume it more likely that a liberal-leaning woman was both a feminist *and* a bank teller rather than simply a bank teller. They called it the "Fallacy of Conjunction."

With this experiment, and a host of others, Kahneman and Tversky exposed a sort of tic in our mental machinery: we're deeply affected by vivid, available evidence, to such a degree that we're willing to make judgments that violate simple logic. We over-conclude based on the available information. We have no trouble packaging in unrelated factors if they happen to occur in proximity to what we already believe.

The Linda problem was later criticized as the psychologists setting their test subjects up for failure. If it was stated in a different way, subjects did not always make the error. But this of course was their point. If we present the evidence in a certain light, the brain malfunctions. It doesn't weigh out the variables in a rational way.

What does this have to do with Hanlon's Razor? The connection is this:

Honorius.
384-423 - Western Roman Emperor for 30 years. His reign was
chaotic and messy, and saw Rome
being sacked for the first time in
almost 800 years.

*

Stilicho.
359-408 - High ranking general in
the Roman army. Half Vandal, his
regency for Honorius marked the
high point of Germanic advance-
ment in the service of Rome.

1

Wilde, Oscar.
"The Critic as Artist, Part 2."
Intentions. London: Heinemann
and Balestier, 1891.

2

Heather, Peter.
*The Fall of the Roman Empire: A
New History of Rome and the Bar-
barians*. Oxford: Oxford University
Press, 2006.

3

Gibbon, Edward.
*The Decline and Fall of the Roman
Empire*, New York: Everyman's
Library, 1910.

When we see something we don't like happen and which
seems wrong, we assume it's intentional. But it's more likely
that it's completely unintentional. Assuming someone is doing
wrong and doing it purposefully is like assuming Linda is more
likely to be a bank teller *and* a feminist. Most people doing
wrong are not bad people trying to be malicious.

With such vividness, and the associated emotional
response, comes a sort of malfunctioning in our minds when
we're trying to diagnose the causes of a bad situation. That's
why we need Hanlon's Razor as an important remedy. Failing
to prioritize stupidity over malice causes things like paranoia.
Always assuming malice puts you at the center of everyone
else's world. This is an incredibly self-centered approach to
life. In reality, for every act of malice, there is almost certainly
far more ignorance, stupidity, and laziness.

«One is tempted to define man as a rational
animal who always loses his temper when he
is called upon to act in accordance with the
dictates of reason.»

Oscar Wilde [1]

The end of an empire

In 408 AD, Honorius* was the Emperor of the Western Roman
Empire. He assumed malicious intentions on the part of his
best General, Stilicho*, and had him executed. According to
some historians, this execution may have been a key factor in
the collapse of the Empire.[2,3]

Why? Stilicho was an exceptional military general who
won many campaigns for Rome. He was also very loyal to the
Empire. He was not, however, perfect. Like all people, he made
some decisions with negative outcomes. One of these was per-
suading the Roman Senate to accede to the demands of Alaric,

Rome didn't fall in a day. It was a decades-long crumble that saw a disbursement of power in Europe and a steady dismantling of the Roman infrastructure.

leader of the Visigoths. Alaric had attacked the Empire multiple times and was no favorite in Rome. They didn't want to give in to his threats and wanted to fight him.

Stilicho counseled against this. Perhaps he had a relationship with Alaric and thought he could convince him to join forces and push back against the other invaders Rome was dealing with. Regardless of his reasoning, this action of Stilicho's compromised his reputation.

Honorius was thus persuaded of the undesirability of having Stilicho around. Instead of defending him, or giving him the benefit of the doubt on the Alaric issue, Honorius assumed malicious intent behind Stilicho's actions—that he wanted the throne and so was making decisions to shore up his power. Honorius ordered the general's arrest and likely supported his execution.

Without Stilicho to influence the relationship with the Goths, the Empire became a military disaster. Alaric sacked Rome two years later, the first barbarian to capture the city in nearly eight centuries. Rome was thus compromised, a huge contributing factor to the collapse of the Western Roman Empire.

Hanlon's Razor, when practiced diligently as a counter to confirmation bias, empowers us, and gives us far more realistic and effective options for remedying bad situations. When we assume someone is out to get us, our very natural instinct is to take actions to defend ourselves. It's harder to take advantage of, or even see, opportunities while in this defensive mode because our priority is saving ourselves—which tends to reduce our vision to dealing with the perceived threat instead of examining the bigger picture.

By not assuming the worst, Vasili Arkhipov single-handedly
avoided nuclear war with the Americans.

*
Arkhipov, Vasili.
1926-1998 - Russian. Retired as a
Vice-Admiral in the Soviet Navy.
In 1961 he was deputy command-
er of K-19. The events on board
inspired the Harrison Ford movie,
K-19: The Widowmaker.

1
Roberts, Priscilla.
*Cuban Missile Crisis: The Essential
Reference Guide.* Santa Barbara:
ABC-CLIO, 2012.

The man who saved the world

On October 27, 1962, Vasili Arkhipov[*] stayed calm, didn't assume malice, and saved the world. Seriously.

This was the height of the Cuban missile crisis. Tensions were high between the United States and the Soviet Union. The world felt on the verge of nuclear war, a catastrophic outcome for all.

American destroyers and Soviet subs were in a standoff in the waters off Cuba. Although they were technically in International waters, the Americans had informed the Soviets that they would be dropping blank depth charges to force the Soviet submarines to surface. The problem was, Soviet HQ had failed to pass this information along, so the subs in the area were ignorant of the planned American action.[1]

Arkhipov was an officer aboard Soviet sub B-59—a sub that, unbeknownst to the Americans, was carrying a nuclear weapon. When the depth charges began to detonate above them, the Soviets on board B-59 assumed the worst. Convinced that war had broken out, the captain of the sub wanted to arm and deploy the nuclear-tipped torpedo.

This would have been an unprecedented disaster. It would have significantly changed the world as we know it, with both the geopolitical and nuclear fallout affecting us for decades. Luckily for us, the launch of the torpedo required all three senior officers on board to agree, and Arkhipov didn't. Instead of assuming malice, he stayed calm and insisted on surfacing to contact Moscow.

Although the explosions around the submarine could have been malicious, Arkhipov realized that to assume so would put the lives of billions in peril. Far better to suppose mistakes and ignorance, and base the decision not to launch on that. In doing so, he saved the world.

They surfaced and returned to Moscow. Arkhipov wasn't hailed as a hero until the record was declassified 40 years later, when documents revealed just how close the world had come to nuclear war.

The Devil Fallacy

Robert Heinlein's character Doc Graves describes the Devil Fallacy in the 1941 sci-fi story "Logic of Empire", as he explains the theory to another character:

"I would say you've fallen into the commonest fallacy of all in dealing with social and economic subjects—the 'devil' theory. You have attributed conditions to villainy that simply result from stupidity.... You think bankers are scoundrels. They are not. Nor are company officials, nor patrons, nor the governing classes back on earth. Men are constrained by necessity and build up rationalizations to account for their acts."

Hanlon's Razor is a great tool for overcoming this fallacy, one we all fall into at one time or another.

As useful as it can be, it is, however, important not to overthink this model. Hanlon's Razor is meant to help us perceive stupidity or error, and their inadvertent consequences. It says that of all possible motives behind an action, the ones that require the least amount of energy to execute (such as ignorance or laziness) are more likely to occur than one that requires active malice.

Conclusion

Ultimately, Hanlon's Razor demonstrates that there are fewer true villains than you might suppose—what people are is human, and like you, all humans make mistakes and fall into traps of laziness, bad thinking, and bad incentives. Our lives are easier, better, and more effective when we recognize this truth and act accordingly. — Sidebar: The Devil Fallacy

Afterthoughts

Congratulations on picking up *The Great Mental Models, Vol. 1*. I like this book for making me smarter, and love it because it's like a glorious idea buffet you can dip into whenever and however you want. You can read it like any other book, from beginning to end. But you can also read it your own way, leaping from section to section as you might navigate a website. Which makes sense, given Shane's origins as a blogger.

That parallel is not mere coincidence. The web changes people. It's changed not just how we buy books, but how we understand, consume, and create art.

The web was a truly new thing in human history when Tim Berners-Lee unveiled it (and I fell in love with it) in the 1990s. The unparalleled freedom and empowerment it brings to millions of voices and businesses today is why I continue to believe in the open web—and why I work at a company that shares my belief.

That company is Automattic. A place which, among other things, brings you WordPress.com, the service that makes it easy to use WordPress—the platform for one-third of all sites on the web. Few internet companies touch so many lives. No internet company works harder to make the web a place where every voice may be heard, and every business earns an equal chance to succeed.

At Automattic, we believe so hard in the web that our corporate headquarters are nowhere and everywhere. When you work with us, you do your thing during hours that work for you, in a location you love. Like your home, for instance.

I hope you enjoy *The Great Mental Models, Vol. 1* and dip into it often in years to come. And, if you're the kind of person I suspect you are—super-smart, super-nice, and committed to an open web for all—I hope you'll join my friends and me at Automattic. A better place to make the web a better place.

https://automattic.com/gmm

Jeffrey Zeldman,
Principal & Creative Director, WordPress.com Special Projects

Acknowledgements

I'm forever indebted to Charlie Munger, Peter Kaufman, Warren Buffett, and Peter Bevelin, who, to varying degrees, started me down the path of multidisciplinary thinking. I owe them a huge debt of gratitude. While I've sought wisdom from the world, it's a journey that one starts and never completes.

When I first started learning about multidisciplinary thinking there was no source of collected wisdom—no place where I could find the big ideas from multiple disciplines in one place. This book, and indeed, this series, is meant to bring some of the big invariant ideas into the world to help us better understand the world we live in and how it interconnects. These pages are filled with ideas from many great minds. It's only fair to point out that any idea you found in this book comes from someone else.

This book would not be here without the work and talents of Rhiannon Beaubien, Morgwn Rimel, Marcia Mihotich, and Garvin Hirt.

I have many friends to thank for reading the manuscript and offering thoughtful and critical feedback for which I'm grateful. Thank you Zachary Smith, Devon Anderson, Jeff Annello, Simon Hørup Eskildsen, Laurence Endersen, and Paul Ciampa.

I want to thank Néna Rawdah for helping edit this from a manuscript into a book.

I also want to thank my kids, William and Mackenzie, who, without knowing it, have provided me with a renewed sense of curiosity and understanding. This book is for you.

I hope you pull this book off your shelf whenever you're stuck or need inspiration in understanding our world. It's designed to be a reference book of big ideas but also a book that pulls you in aesthetically through the intersection of design and content.

Shane

Picture Credits

In order of appearance:

1. Heracles: Sergej Razvodovskij/Shutterstock.com

2. Bloodletting: Aldobrandino of Siena, Li Livres dou Santé (Blood letting), late 13th Century/Wikipedia

3. Old map: Fra Maura (original), W. Fraser (this reproduction), World Map, 1450 (original), 1806 (this reproduction)/Wikipedia

4. Sykes-Picot line: Royal Geographical Society, Mark Sykes and Francois Georges-Picot, Sykes-Picot Line, 1916/Wikipedia

5. City Scene: George Bellows, Cliff Dwellers, 1913/Wikipedia

6. Sylvie and Bruno: Harry Furniss, Sylvie and Bruno Concluded, 1893/Wikipedia

7. Tenzing Norgay: Edmund Hillary, Tenzing Norgay on the Summit of Mount Everest, 1953/Royal Geographical Society

8. Car/mechanic: ESB Professional/Shutterstock.com

9. Elizabeth I: Anonymous, Queen Elizabeth I of England in Coronation Robes, c.1600/Wikipedia

10. Carpet: Polad Gasimov/Shutterstock.com

11. Lebron James: Jason Miller, Lebron James at Cleveland Cavaliers Media Day, 2017/Getty Images Sport

12. Woody Allen: Mike Marsland, 'Cafe Society' Photocall - The 69th Annual Cannes Film Festival, 2016/WireImage

13. Archduke car: Stefan97, Heeresgeschichtliches Museum Wien Attentat in Sarajevo Auto, 2017/Wikipedia

14. Bacteria: National Institute of Allergy and Infectious Diseases, Klebsiella pneumoniae Bacteria, 2014/Wikipedia

15. Shadow of a man: Ein business-Mann-silhouette auf den Zehenspitzen Wegsehen – Stockfoto/istockphoto.com

16. Cleopatra: William Wetmore Story, Cleopatra, 1878/Wikipedia

17. Hands shaking: prince_apple/Shutterstock.com

18. Ice cream: Good Ice Cream/Wallpaperget.com

19. Black swan: Potapov Alexander/Shutterstock.com

20. Sabotage poster: Artist unknown from Office for Emergency Management, Sabotage Can Outweigh Production, 1941-1945/Wikipedia

21. French poster: Artist unknown in the UK, La liberté pour la France ... les libertés pour les Français, 1940/Wikipedia

22. Legs: Vladimir Gjorgiev/Shutterstock.com

23. Sherlock Holmes: Sidney Paget, A Scandal in Bohemia, 1891/Wikipedia

24. Lucky Strike poster: American Tabaco Company, To keep a slender figure No one can deny, 1929/thesocietypages.org

25. CCTV: Phonlamai Photo/Shutterstock.com

26. Nightingale chart: Florence Nightingale, Diagram of the causes of mortality in the army in the East, 1858/Wikipedia

27. Andromeda Galaxy: NASA/JPL-Caltech, Andromeda Galaxy, 2017/NASA website

28. Zebra: prapass/Shutterstock.com

29. Computer: Rik Myslewski, Ibm pcjr with display, 2014/Wikipedia

30. Rome: Thomas Cole, Destruction from The Course of Empire, 1836/Wikipedia

31. B59 sub: US Navy, Soviet b-59 submarine, 1962/Wikipedia

32. Banker: Everett Collections/Shutterstock.com